PROTECT YOURSELF

Robert G. Barthol, an instructor at Chabot College, Hayward, California, is a retired FBI agent and has been teaching self-defense to men and women, both law-enforcement and civilian, for 34 years.

PROTECT YOURSELF

A SELF-DEFENSE GUIDE FOR WOMEN FROM PREVENTION TO COUNTER-ATTACK

ROBERT G. BARTHOL

A SPECTRUM BOOK

Prentice-Hall, Inc., Englewood Cliffs, New Jersey 07632

Library of Congress Cataloging in Publication Data

Barthol, Robert G
    Protect yourself.

    (A Spectrum Book)
    Includes index.
    1. Self-defense for women.   I. Title.
GV1111.5.B35   796.8′1   79-880
ISBN 0-13-731430-2
ISBN 0-13-731422-1 pbk.

A Spectrum Book

10 9 8 7 6 5 4 3 2 1

Editorial/production supervision
and interior design by Eric Newman
Page layout by Charles H. Pelletreau
Cover design by Len Leoni, Jr.
Manufacturing buyer: Cathie Lenard

Prentice-Hall International, Inc., *London*
Prentice-Hall of Australia Pty. Limited, *Sydney*
Prentice-Hall of Canada, Ltd., *Toronto*
Prentice-Hall of India Private Limited, *New Delhi*
Prentice-Hall of Japan, Inc., *Tokyo*
Prentice-Hall of Southeast Asia Pte. Ltd., *Singapore*
Whitehall Books Limited, *Wellington, New Zealand*

To the Bad Guys, who made this book necessary.

CONTENTS

THANKS...

To my wife, Jane, for her understanding and forebearance while I spent the many necessary hours preparing this book and working (?) with pretty young women. (She also typed and proofread, and she even fed me.)

To Carol Chervier, my illustrator, reader, helper, suggester, encourager, and forthright (and, unfortunately, devastatingly accurate) critic.

To Beth Doolittle, Director, Marin Rape Crisis Center, and expert teacher of these methods, for the checking of the methods, the testing of the explanations, and keen observing of the photographs.

To my lovely and talented models who posed for the photographs herein: Terry Harris, Sue Anne Barthol, Coralee Barthol, Rita Roth, and Debbie Neill.

To my bleary-eyed typists: Susie Barthol, Mary Cuthbertson, and Dianne Burnett.

To the very capable Chad Reeser, my photographer.

To the long list of friends who went over the various drafts and commented, criticized, and suggested.

PROTECT YOURSELF

INTRODUCTION

"How to" articles on self-defense for women have long featured illustrations depicting a 102-pound girl casually knocking a muscular bully to the ground or sending him fleeing in terror. Let me set the record straight: As a result of reading this (or any other book), you will *not* be able to reduce a 252-pound defensive tackle to a whimpering cripple with a quick flick of your wrist. You might with a hand grenade, but *not* with a quick flick of your wrist. The book you're looking for is *Wonder Woman* comics!

You've pinned a lot of faith on the claims made in the many courses and books on self-defense for women, so this opening statement may disappoint you. However, it is an honest statement, probably the first completely honest one you've heard on this subject. With this book, I intend to make you face reality and not be misled by the prettied-up TV versions of attacks and defenses. Beware of dramatic exhibitions put on by instructors in this field! Anyone with normal reflexes can learn to put on a play, and with a trained and cooperative partner, anyone can make almost any attack or defense, however inept and worthless, look easy and foolproof. Many techniques work beautifully in a gym against a cooperative, nonaggressive partner who renders his "attack" in slow motion. The test is, will the technique work under actual combat conditions against a strong, aggressive antagonist?

Let's face it: If we consider nothing else, by nature's design (unfair though it may be), the male of the species is bigger and stronger than the female. If you believe you're going to knock your opponent cold with a well-placed blow, consider this: Lightweight professional boxers rarely knock out their opponents in their *own* weight class, let alone a heavyweight. How can an untrained woman do what a professional boxer can't? It is a well-proven fact that a good big man will whip a good little man. Then think about this: Since he was five or six years old, the average male has spent thousands of hours developing his muscles, reflexes, timing, and offensive and defensive skills through football, baseball, boxing, wrestling, running, and fighting. You probably have misspent your formative years playing with dolls and learning to cook and sew. (You mean girls don't do that anymore? Okay—I'll bet not many play football, either!) Although you can't make up those thousands of hours by reading a self-defense book, you *can* learn techniques that can save you from rape, injury, disfigurement, or even death.

This book is *not* a course in judo, kung fu, karate, or jiu jitsu, which, for real proficiency, require hundreds of hours of arduous practice, but it does contain some elements of these martial arts and many other skills. Self-defense for women is a series of surprise moves, well rehearsed and done quickly and with good body mechanics, designed to catch your bigger and stronger opponent off guard. Ordinarily you will not kill or disable, or you may not even hurt your opponent. But you will get loose, at least momentarily.

You need so much more than "holds," "throws," "defense," or "counters." Simply showing you all the tricks is like showing a big, strong man all the moves in boxing and then shoving him into the ring. Even a mediocre boxer will massacre him. Sure, our strong man knows the technical moves, but he doesn't know how to deliver his blows effectively, how to take advantage of openings, how to get the maximum power into his punches, and he hasn't learned to read the signs tipping off an attack by his opponent fast enough to be able to set up his defenses. He also does not know how to put combinations of punches and footwork together to finish the job. What good does it do to break a choke hold, for example, and then simply stand there and let your attacker reapply the choke or some other hold?

Stress training

Although the techniques in this book can be learned in far less time than it takes to learn the formal martial arts, there are no shortcuts. The casual reader who skims through this book, picking up a technique here and there without learning the basic skills that must precede it, will be disappointed with the results. First, you must learn the basic principles. Then you learn the techniques, step by step, practicing them until they become conditioned reflexes. Finally, you perform them "under stress," and, if practical, under combat conditions.

"Under stress." Right here much of the training of women falls apart. Most males are used to stress conditions from their participation in athletics: Loud noises, menacing gestures, and shouted threats will probably evoke a grin and appropriate retort, and a sudden attack will bring an immediate and automatic defense and counterattack. Few women have had this training. On a few occasions I have been faced by a woman, some claiming a black belt in one of the martial arts, who proclaimed she was thoroughly trained and my equal in the art of self-defense. When I have been unable to explain to her why she is not, I have a favorite gambit that has worked every time I have had to use it. I say, "Let's try it," and as we are walking onto the mat, I suddenly turn, with hands over my head like Dracula, and, screaming like a banshee, rush down upon her. In every case she covered her face and recoiled; one "victim" even fell down before I reached her. None of these women even attempted to defend herself.

This is not a "put down" of women. My point is that all the training in the world is worthless if you are not used to reacting under stress. These competent women had been trained under laboratory conditions in a gymnasium with a cooperative partner and were simply panicked by the noise, surprise, and violence of my attack. Under real emergency conditions, your chances are zero if you panic. However, fear is normal, and the flow of adrenalin inspired by that fear is the best thing that you can have, for it makes you faster, stronger, less sensitive to pain, and more able to cope with the danger. Practice under stress will reduce the chance of this crippling fear or panic.

Lethal and nonlethal defenses

Most books and courses in women's self-defense concentrate almost exclusively on methods against the rapist or assassin—lethal defenses to kill or maim the assailant. However, you also need defenses for the more common situations in which lethal force is not desired, such as when you are "defending your honor" in a parked car or in your apartment against a man who was merely a date until that moment. With the aid of too many drinks, he has decided to take by force (but rarely all-out force) what he couldn't get permission to have. This is a guy you'll see at the office tomorrow, or who will phone you as soon as he's sober with an embarrassed and contrite apology. You wouldn't dream of putting out his eye, permanently destroying his manhood with a knee, or clobbering him with a heavy glass ashtray. So we'll also describe some less painful and less permanent techniques for him.

My experience as a law-enforcement officer has convinced me that many people set themselves up to become victims, sometimes in all innocence, through their own ignorance or carelessness, so I will first teach a far less dramatic art—how to avoid getting into situations that might require physical force to get out of. The first half of this book is devoted to common-sense approaches to your daily routines, to preventive actions, and to methods of escaping from or avoiding danger without physical contact. The second part is devoted to the physical actions and counters you can use to defend yourself and to escape the clutches of an attacker.

CHAPTER
ONE

PREVENTIVE
TECHNIQUES

Earlier I mentioned that my experience has taught me that many of the bad or embarrassing situations people get into are at least partly of their own making. Many times women do not realize that they are setting themselves up for a problem or fail to take elementary precautions that might have avoided the problem in the first place. As a prime example, consider an action that is incomprehensible to me: In spite of overwhelming evidence of the deadly danger therein, some women still set themselves up by hitchhiking. Women who hitchhike are simply not facing today's world. They use the philosophy "It won't happen to me." Talk to them afterward—those who can talk—and they have the same refrain: "I just couldn't believe anyone could do such a thing!" What they refuse to believe is that weirdos and psychopaths regard these young women standing by the side of the street or highway as a smorgasbord set out for their inspection. They cruise around and pick the one they want, *and their intention at the time they pick her up* is rape or murder. Read your newspaper—and remember that only about one rape in ten is reported. Some district attorneys have actually refused to prosecute in rape cases because the victim was hitchhiking!

There is another side of this coin. Don't *you* pick up hitchhikers. Surveys by various police agencies universally reveal that an amazing percentage of hitchhikers are ex-convicts, wanted men, or people who have mental problems of varying degrees. In short, the same kind of weirdo who picks up unwary hitchhiking women also is on the side of the road hitchhiking. By stopping and letting him into your car, you are providing the time, place, and transportation for a rape, robbery, kidnapping, or murder. How thoughtful of you! Another disturbing recent development is that often an attractive young woman will be hitchhiking, and when the motorist stops (it may be you, because you're not afraid of a lone young woman!) one or more males come out of the shrubbery or ditch to join her. Some of our more gruesome crimes have come out of this gambit recently. Don't stop. A young woman can be just as dangerous as a man (read your newspapers). Often a girl will accept a ride home or an escort to her car from a casual pickup in a bar, a dance, or even a house party. Ask any policeman handling the sex-crimes detail.

The way to avoid these problems is obvious. Don't hitch-hike. Don't accept rides from strangers or casual acquaintances. I wish I could get every woman who does either of these things to listen to the sobbing story of a victim of the same situation, who will live with the terrifying memory of it, the shame of it, and maybe the permanent physical injuries from it, for the rest of her life.

Prevention

The above situations are the easy ones to prevent. Just don't do them! But I'm also talking about the attempted rape or attack on the street at night while you're walking to or from your car or bus, walking the dog, walking to the supermarket, or simply walking. I'm talking about the assault in the home when a burglar or other intruder has sneaked or broken in. I'm talking about the kidnap and rape when some man suddenly opens your car door and slides in beside you, forcing you to drive away with him. I'm talking about the man who gains entrance to your home posing as a salesman or repairman, or who asks to use your phone or bathroom. I'm talking about the guy who hides in the back seat of your car when you go into the store and kidnaps you when you re-enter the car. You can come up with dozens more—and they've all happened and are happening with frightening regularity (read your newspaper). Unfortunately, more and more of these situations are ending up in murder. Unlike hitchhiking and accepting rides, these situations are not so easily dealt with. We'll discuss them separately and at length in later chapters.

The general safety rule is: *Don't put yourself in a situation in which the assault might happen.* Don't expect a simple answer to cover all situations, and I know that there will be times when you have no choice but to be out alone at night. Just use your head. Arrange your errands for the daylight hours whenever possible. If you work late at the office, have a male fellow employee escort you to your car and see you safely started—you might even drive him back to the office. If you're leaving someone's home, use the male of the house or a fellow male guest whom you can trust to handle the escort duty to your car. You may not know it, but you often make points by feeding the male ego because we males love to be thought of as protectors. Don't turn down the legitimate offer of an escort by saying, "Oh, I'm not afraid." Even if it is true, use common sense and play the percentages.

Another simple precaution is to go in a group. In the car situation, you all walk to the nearest of the cars, all get in and drive in turn to the other cars, standing by in the locked car until each one dropped off gets started and away. The feeling of security in these cases is worth the trouble.

Social situations

Another general category we might call "social." This is the type of situation that might arise at the end of a date, such as when the date isn't satisfied with a polite handshake and a simple "Goodbye." The physical action may start before you get out of the car, or after he takes you into your apartment, or at the drive-in movie, or when he parks to "look at the lights" (and it turns out that that wasn't what he really had in mind at all). And so on.

In the "social" setup, make sure you're not telegraphing a message to your escort that you don't mean. An excellent book, *Body Language*, by Julius Fast, explains this in detail. Simplified, it means that by the way you act, stand, talk, sit, respond—in fact, by everything you do—you are sending messages to the other person as to what you are and what you want. If you sit touching or very close to a man in a car, he is going to read that as an invitation for future advances. If you've given him the "come on" all evening, don't expect to turn him off like a light switch when you decide to take your leave.

This does not mean you can't be natural and affectionate; nor am I advocating a paranoid approach to your social life. It is simply that there will be occasions when you will be faced with a situation in which the male may not be willing to accept your decision that the evening is over. You must have some effective escape gambits learned for these situations. If you read signs that indicate you are shortly going to be a participant in an amorous wrestling match you don't desire, plan a quick goodbye and exit when he drives you home. Be on your side of the seat, have your key in your hand, and have the door open as soon as he stops. Short of leaping on you as a spider would on a fly, he is stuck. He's not likely to try the same tactics on the sidewalk that he would in the privacy of his car. If he insists on coming in after the date and you don't want him to, an imaginary roommate or mother asleep in the apartment has been success-fully used in the past. The general rule is: If you don't trust him, don't get yourself in a position such that you are alone with him. If you do decide to trust him and something happens, that's when your assertiveness training and the rest of the defenses discussed later in this book come in.

Probably the single error that sets up most of the social situations is that of being too nice, by failing to say "No!" clearly and definitely when the action you don't want first starts. The words "I don't think I'd better," "You shouldn't do that," or other indefinite words are going to be read as maidenly shyness, which you both expect to be overcome by his manly aggressiveness, since you can't appear to be too eager. He now takes further steps, confident of your reaction, and suddenly you have to fend off a more definite pass—which is going to irk him somewhat. A firm "no" at the outset will prevent many an unpleasant situation and make much "self-defense" unnecessary.

Lest you go too far in thinking in terms of physical action, let me throw in a word or two of practical advice. Physical resistance is the last resort. Prevention is the easiest course, with talking and trickery next. Then, if all else fails, you go into action. By the very fact that you didn't get physical at the outset, the male has been lulled into a sense of security, so that when you do erupt, he is caught by surprise, giving you a good chance of success.

Also, starting a fight while a knife is at your throat is silly. Brave, but silly. And possibly fatal. Use your head! This is not a book of magic tricks.

CHAPTER TWO
ASSERTIVENESS

Teaching women self-defense, as well as researching actual attacks on women, made one thing abundantly clear to me: When confronted with a real-life dangerous or unpleasant situation, even with an expert's knowledge of self-defense, most women fail to use their knowledge and training. This applies whether the problem is an attempted rape or an aggressive male's subjecting them to an unwanted pawing at a party. It springs from the psychological conditioning of women from infancy to be "nice." They are taught "Don't be rude," "Don't be physical," "Women are weak," "I will just get hurt," "Men are too powerful to fight against," "Don't make a scene." This has engendered a philosophy such that women are unwilling to believe that someone might actually want to hurt them, that they shouldn't be suspicious of everyone. As a result, we find women often helplessly trying to fend off the pawing male at a party with a nervous giggle and an apologetic tone; they will often submit passively to the unwanted caresses when their feeble, nonthreatening push-offs and squirmings and nonangry protestations are ignored. In the more violent encounters, women tend to cave in when faced by unexpected violence. Unfortunately, this happens more often than not.

Past conditioning

There are three main facets to this problem. First, women's conditioning effectively prevents them from acting positively in this kind of an emergency. Second, actual physical fear has a paralyzing effect on their will to resist. Third, there is a little-recognized but most dangerous offshoot of this fear reaction: The projection of that fear to the viewer by their body language actually makes them a more likely target. The rapist and attacker prefer to pick on the weak and helpless, and if you project that image of yourself, your danger is intensified. By the same token, the more capable and confident you appear (and that may be Academy Award acting!), the less attractive a target you look to him.

Fortunately, there are solutions, many of which lie in the realm of psychology. You are faced with the monumental task of changing your life-long conditioning, without the help of a psychiatrist or a trained counselor. All you have is this book. However, an open mind that accepts the unpleasant fact that these conditions do exist, and a serious effort to make the specific changes suggested hereafter, can result in your repro-gramming yourself to have a more positive reaction to danger. This could, in an extreme emergency, quite literally mean the difference between life and death.

Outward appearance of fear

As stated earlier, prevention is the easiest and most suc-cessful self-defense. We will start that defense by learning the outward appearance of fear—the body language that betrays you to your enemy. Watch an untrained, passively conditioned woman walking past a male or group of males who might be a threat, or even walking alone on a dark and deserted street. Note how fear looks! Hunched shoulders. Fast, nervous walk. Eyes averted—she carefully avoids looking at anyone, and especially never catching anyone's eyes. Body stiff in its move-ments. Arms may be folded or she may be hugging herself. Hands may be hidden in her pockets. Tiptoeing, trying not to make any noise. Head down. In her mind she has the irrational hope that maybe no one will notice her!

That is how she looks to an observer. Now let's see how this fear looks and feels from the *inside*. Shallow, fast breathing. Neck and face feel stiff. Shoulders feel tight. An overwhelming urge to break into a run. A tendency to talk silently—or even out loud—to oneself. A feeling of panic and an urge to cry. What a terrible way to feel!

Reprogramming
your conditioning

You now have the job of breaking your prior passive conditioning and easing some of your fears, many of which are caused by that conditioning. When you feel insecure and afraid, that physically affects your body functions and is reflected in your body language. Are you aware that we can reverse this process by deliberately sending the impulses in the other direction, from the body to the mind? By means of a few physical tricks, you can program your body and body language to reflect the attitude of a winner rather than a loser, and your mind actually accepts this! As a result, you *feel* like a winner, and your fears and insecurities disappear or are greatly lessened. The freedom from fear alone is a major victory, but the practical result is that a would-be attacker is now going to read you differently and may reconsider.

To start this reprogramming, think back to the discussion of what fear looks like to the observer and how it feels from the inside. We will set out to change the physical manifestations of that fear and make our mind accept what it now feels. The steps are ridiculously easy, so easy that you may think they are too simple to work. They do work!

Step 1. *Breathe.* Remember this one word when you are moving into, or find yourself in, a situation that is a fearful one for you. The situation can range from going in to see your boss for a raise or breaking a date with a boyfriend, to a really dangerous physical situation. Deliberately take a couple of deep breaths and then consciously breathe so that you can hear yourself and can feel the air going to your lungs. The oxygen will keep your brain alert and your muscles ready, and you can *feel* a sense of power fill you. You can test this right now. Try it!

Step 2. *Walk erect, head high.* Listen to and feel your feet hitting the ground. It gives you a feeling of control, gives you better balance, and keeps you from tiptoeing and looking scared.

Step 3. *Relax!* Whether standing or walking, move your body freely. Stiffness is part of the look of fear. If you are walking, consciously swing your arms. You've seen athletes confidently

19

striding along, swinging their arms, their bodies free and relaxed. This is what you want to look like.

Step 4. *Consciously* move your head and eyes, taking in the environment around you. This is the look of alertness and awareness. *Actively look for what you are afraid of!* Fear of the unknown is one of the most paralyzing of all fears, and looking the other way will *not* make the danger go away. Confront your fears head on. If there really is no problem, you have saved yourself some frightening and self-humiliating moments. If it turns out that there is a problem, the sooner you know about it the more time you have to avoid it or formulate a plan of action.

The only way these techniques will become a part of you is to use them constantly. But why use them only for an emergency? They will work in your daily life! Use them to build your confidence and self-esteem. The next time you go walking, put them into practice. I guarantee you will feel better, and I'll bet that after a while people will notice a change and respond to you in a more positive way.

In short, this is a method of taking control of your life. If you are going to daydream and fantasize (and we all do), make yourself a winner in your fantasies. Isn't it silly to scare yourself to death with visions of terror, defeat, and humiliation? Next time you start anticipating all the terrible things that could happen to you, consciously swing from the ''loser'' to the ''winner'' image. Slowly but surely that winner image will become part of you in reality. Try it!

Barthol's Law

Now that you're projecting this positive body language, we'll work on amplifying it. First, let's take a realistic look at the situation that exists if there is an attack or a threatened attack on you. In the first place, *you* are the wronged one. *You* did not start the problem. You owe your attacker *nothing!* If worst comes to worst, whose welfare is more important, his or yours? In teaching law enforcement officers how to avoid injury or death, I state what I call *Barthol's Law*. This comes into play when I am confronted with a situation, not of my choice, in which I have to defend myself, in which the bad guy is about to do something to hurt me if I don't get to him first. "Barthol's Law" simply states: "If it comes to a choice between thee and me, it's gonna be *thee!*" It means that you resolve all doubts in *your* favor. If anyone gets hurt, it's going to be the attacker. Harden yourself to this attitude *before* you are confronted with the necessity of action. My experience with women in self-defense has shown that many of you are so reluctant to hurt anyone that you won't attack the attacker and thereby end up a victim, sometimes a dead one. This is that conditioning we've been discussing. Don't *be* a victim. The hell with him! *He* started it! That's Barthol's Law!

A very common reaction in women when they are the victims of an unprovoked assault is that they, in spite of all logic and against all common sense, feel guilty and apologetic. This is especially true of sexual-assault victims. Their anger is directed against themselves, not against the attacker. This has been proven true in cases running the entire gamut from an unwanted pawing at a party or on a date to an actual assault or rape.

In some of the social situations in which women are being pawed and are struggling to fend off unwanted attentions, one of the most common reactions is that the woman smiles and giggles while struggling and protesting! She certainly doesn't *feel* like smiling, and may actually be in fear, but smile she does. Numerous interviews with women indicate that most are not aware they are smiling. When we discuss it, most attribute it to a sense of guilt, as if they were responsible for the man's attentions. I know it doesn't make sense, but nonetheless it is true.

Get mad!

Women must reprogram themselves to get rid of this conditioning and learn to get mad—fighting mad—when confronted by a situation in which someone has invaded their personal space. If they are molested in a public place, many women struggle silently, too embarrassed to speak out. This is the time to speak out loudly and clearly, with undisguised anger in your voice and face, and tell the creep off. He is counting on your "nice" programming to let him get away unscathed. Fool him. Speak out and watch him disappear back into the woodwork. You will still be as feminine and gentle as you were before; you don't give up the right to these qualities because you defend yourself. The time to handle these situations is now, before they happen. Make a vow to get mad. The best way to ensure that you will is to role play the situations now. Have a male or female friend take the part of a man who is the aggressor. The simplest situation is one in which the male, a stranger, is merely pushy and won't take no for an answer when he is asking for a date, wants to sit down at your table, won't quit asking personal questions (like "What's your name?" "Where do you live?" "Where do you work?" "Do you have a boyfriend?" and so on). No matter how much you indicate that you are not interested and want to be left alone, he keeps persisting, and you keep answering because you are afraid of being rude and hurting his feelings. Balderdash! He is *counting* on that reaction. In this role playing, some of you are going to find it very difficult to firmly and definitely say "No" or "Leave me alone!" even to your friends who are playing the part of the obnoxious creep. In situations like these, it is *your* peace that is being disturbed, *your* privacy that is being invaded. If your polite turndowns do not send him away, then you have the absolute *right* to be rude, even insulting. Remember Barthol's Law. *He* caused your unpleasant reaction, not you. Strip him of the protection your conditioning used to afford him. Take control of your life—don't give it to somebody else by default. Fortunately, after role playing a few times, it becomes easier and easier, and the ability will stay with you for later use in a real-life situation.

Anger, fear, and panic are some of the emotions that cause adrenalin to shoot into your bloodstream. This little trick of nature's made it possible for us to be here, because our caveman ancestors never would have survived without it. Adrenalin coursing through our veins makes actual physical changes in us: Our vision and hearing become more acute, our muscles stronger, our reactions faster, and our pain threshold gets so high that we might not even notice a blow or injury that would normally incapacitate us. This gave the caveman the extra energy needed to outrun or outfight the saber-toothed tiger (whose attitude bears more than a passing resemblance to that of the guy who is forcing his attentions on you). Your assignment is to learn how to make sure that this adrenalin's effect is *anger* rather than fear or panic. Change your conditioning! From this time forward, consciously think *anger* when you are imposed upon. Practice showing it in your face. Wipe that smile off! Narrow your eyes. Grit your teeth. Hiss or snarl your command to *"Leave me alone!"* A mirror is great to practice with. (Try not to practice while walking down the street under normal conditions. A woman contorting her face into rage and anger and hissing under these conditions is likely to have the sidewalk entirely to herself.)

Stress training

A word you may have noticed appearing often on these pages is *consciously*. I mean it. By *consciously* and *deliberately* practicing these techniques and thinking about them, you set up conditioned reflexes, habit–patterns that become part of you and will almost automatically spring into use when you need them. It is especially important to work at setting up your conditioned reflexes in this area, because you have to override your previously established reflexes. Unfortunately, it is not easy to unlearn something that is deeply ingrained. Let me give you an example from my field. Consider a right-handed law-enforcement officer who has carried his sidearm in a cross-draw holster on his left hip for ten years. He has spent many hours training himself to draw quickly and smoothly and has faced many emergency confrontations in which he has had to fast-draw his weapon. That habit–pattern is set deep in his subconscious; he is *conditioned* to have an effective and fast reaction to a stress situation. Now he decides a right-hand draw is faster and more effective, so he buys a right-hand holster to wear on his right hip and retrains himself to a direct, instead of a cross-draw, technique. He doesn't know it, but he may be in real danger. If a gunman suddenly jumped out at him, the officer, trained to split-second response, would react instinctively, without conscious thought (because conscious thought is too slow in an emergency situation). Unfortunately, he would probably claw for his nonexistent cross-draw holster on his left side—because his stress training over the years had set up those instinctive neurological patterns. In emergencies, we tend to revert to what we originally learned or what we learned under stress. In order for the officer to negate his prior training and reset a new programmed response, he must not only practice the new method over and over, but also practice it under stress. Only then will he automatically react in an emergency along his new training lines.

To get back to your problem: You must learn your new *anger* reaction the same way. Practice it by fantasizing the situations, by practicing in front of the mirror, and by working with friends. Role playing will help to set up more stressful situations and your new habit–pattern will begin to surface automatically. It is as simple as that. If you *consciously* and *deliberately* think about it, practice it, and practice it under stress, the technique is yours to command from now on. Remember this well, because you can use the same method to learn the physical self-defense techniques that follow in this book.

Yelling vs. screaming

Women are told to scream when in danger, and later on, in the chapter "Obtaining Help," we discuss when and where to scream, but let's first consider it here under the "assertiveness" concept. First, compare screaming with yelling. You will need both. Screaming sounds scared. It is high pitched and loud, designed to attract attention and help—to frighten off your attacker, because he now fears help will be arriving and he will be caught or hurt. Yelling, on the other hand, sounds mad! Yelling is a lion roaring, a way of proclaiming your anger, outrage, and willingness to fight to the world in general and to your attacker specifically. Remember our discussion of the attacker's preferring to pick on the weak and helpless? A scream is frightened, therefore weak and easy. A yell is mad, therefore aggressive and active. No easy prey here, but an angry lioness! Sure you're scared, but let's spread it around a little. Scare him in return by your unexpectedly (and it will be unexpected) angry and aggressive attitude. This is more than he bargained for. Research indicates many attempted rapes have been aborted by this very technique. Your assailant is not psychologically prepared for this reversal of roles and often flees in panic. Bank robberies have been thwarted by the teller's simply yelling, "No! Get out of here!" and other endearments. The robbers, counting on weak-kneed compliance, couldn't handle it and took off, mumbling about how they don't make tellers the way they used to. (I do *not* recommend getting tough while a gun is in your face. I'm just illustrating how well aggressiveness can work under even extreme conditions.) An additional benefit to you is that you don't feel nearly as scared and helpless when you yell; the adrenalin flows and your self-esteem rises to new heights. You can also use this in less-than-lethal situations against the persistent masher who won't leave you alone.

Screaming and yelling must be practiced if you want to become efficient in their use. Don't practice in the wrong surroundings where people will think it is for real and try to come to your aid: They might not come next time when you do mean it. You can practice by screaming and yelling into a pillow pressed against your face. You can also practice while driving your car; anyone watching thinks you are singing! (Be sure to have your windows rolled up and refrain while waiting at a stop signal!) Again, I'm recommending a conscious and deliberate practice of a technique so you get good at it.

Let's sum up this chapter. You have certain rights that you should and must exercise. You have the *right* to be suspicious, to control who enters your home or touches your body, to decide how close you want people to come to you. You have the *right* to become rude, obnoxious, or weird to protect yourself.

You must consciously and deliberately reflect your confidence and competence to the observer (and to yourself) by the way you walk, look, and act, by your obvious awareness of your immediate environment and your ability to control it. Shed that scared-rabbit image—go forth like a lioness and take control of your life. The freedom from fear is one of the greatest of our freedoms!

HOME SECURITY AND DEFENSE

Numerous surveys indicate that home security and defense is a prime worry of the average woman, and a look at the crime statistics shows that the worry is more than justified. With the startling rise in home burglaries in the past few years (and over half of home burglaries are now in daylight), the nice, old-fashioned habit of leaving the front door unlocked or a window open for fresh air (where can you get *fresh* air, anyway?) is dangerous, and an open (no pun intended) invitation to the burglar. A screen is *no* protection. To leave the back door unlocked for the milkman is to invite trouble. One of the favorite techniques of the neighborhood burglar is to move around the area looking for unlocked doors and windows—and finding enough of them to keep him in business. It also means that he will usually pass by the houses that are secure—yours, I hope. This technique is also used by your neighborhood rapists, who simply walk in on you. So, locking your doors and windows will prevent the opportunistic entry of the robber or rapist and the easy entrance of the burglar, who, often enough, turns into a rapist when he finds you at home. It also means that if he wants to get in, he has to break in, giving you some chance to frighten him off, escape, call for help, or defend yourself. You've removed his basic principle of surprise.

Prevention

Like all the rest of our defensive techniques, these also start with preventive actions. A lecture on firefighting starts not with how to put out a fire but with how to avoid having the fire in the first place. *Prevention.* It covers the cleaning up of combustible trash, repairing frayed electrical cords, getting rid
29   of explosive liquids, warning of the dangers of cleaning with

gasoline and naphtha, and numerous other suggestions for changes when experience has taught the experts that similar situations have led to fires in the past. It also covers how to plan your escape if a fire does start.

So, we start our discussion on home security and defense the same way—with prevention, the easiest form of self-defense. Not as dramatic as the physical self-defense techniques, but much safer—and far more certain of success.

Let me try to nail something down right here: If you really are concerned about your safety, take these points seriously and *do* something about them. As in the firefighting example above, the experts know from experience which situations have caused problems in the past. If you follow the rules I am laying out here, your chances of being attacked or robbed are cut down drastically. It's that easy. Few of the rules set out are any more difficult or more of a nuisance than those you are following right now. We're merely setting up a different—not a more difficult—routine that is far safer. Why not be sensible and follow it?

Signs of an unoccupied home

Now we go ahead. Although our criminal will roam the area looking for his targets for today or tonight, don't *offer* your home or apartment to him. Normally, the home that appears to be occupied and secure will not be a target. By the same token, the obviously open, unoccupied home will be.

The first thing the burglar looks for are the signs of the unoccupied house. Two or three newspapers or advertising circulars lying around or visible mail tell him the family is away for a while. So does the accumulation of windblown trash around your front and garage doors. He has a trained, professional eye for these things and will read them correctly. The preventive procedure is easy, but you must set it up in advance. First, be sure to stop all papers, milk, or any other kind of delivery. When you are going to be away for a while, have the post office hold your mail so that it doesn't accumulate, particularly if you have a visible mailbox. A slot through which your mail falls into your garage is best, because even today's mail left in the visible box indicates there is probably no one home at the moment. A word of caution here: Note that I said the mail fell through into your *garage*. This is safer than having the slot in your front door or anywhere into your house. The prowler can raise the little metal flap on the mail slot and look right into your home as a Peeping Tom or to see who, if anyone, is at home. He can also listen at the slot to determine the same thing. Sometimes, if the slot is too big or of poor design, he can reach in with his hand or a special tool and unlock the door.

Everyone has at least one neighbor, relative, or friend who could check at least the outside of the house, daily if possible, picking up the trash, circulars, packages left by delivery men, notices of delivery, newspapers (I have stopped the newspaper and found that the carrier delivered for several days before he discontinued), and anything else. Your friend should also make a circuit of the house to make sure that no one has broken in. It is shocking to come home from a vacation and find the house or apartment burglarized. The police are hampered because they have no idea when it was done and no starting place for their investigation. Also, once the house has been broken open, others, possibly children, may use the same broken patio door or window and further vandalize the place.

If your friend or neighbor is one whom you can trust with a key, so much the better. Have your friend also check inside the house, changing the position of the drapes and curtains occasionally, and maybe the timing and position of the lamps that are on automatic timers. By the way, don't close your drapes and draw the curtains while you are away. This is another sign of an unoccupied house.

In passing, I should note that it is a poor idea to have valuable objects visible. Such things as color TVs or expensive stereo or camera equipment should be out of sight of the windows to avoid making a display for the burglar to window-shop before he chooses his victim.

Sometimes the friend gives you a bonus: I have exchanged checkouts with neighbors and have found that they have forgotten open windows, unlocked windows and doors, backyard sprinklers whirling away, water left running in the house, and other little items that I could handle that had nothing to do with burglars, although they might have if left untended.

Another idea is to have a neighbor leave his or her car (locked, of course) parked in your driveway or in front of your house as often as possible. This gives the appearance of somebody's being at home. Another variation of this is to have the neighbor leave a couple of cheap kid's toys by the front door or on the lawn, providing he or she moves them daily.

Either impose on your long-suffering neighbor or hire someone to cut your lawn if you are away for a considerable time. The unkempt lawn is also a sign of extended vacations. While he's at it, he or she might as well turn on the sprinklers and water the shrubbery. Not only will your house look lived in, but while the neighbor is working around there, it will be, in effect, occupied.

Don't ever leave your garage doors open when you drive off, even for a few minutes. An empty garage usually means an empty house, with that house consequently becoming a target. Also, the prowler now has access to at least part of your home and has a better chance to break in unnoticed. He can also steal anything he wants out of your garage, simply by darting in and out, with the elapsed time of one or two minutes. This is a very common form of burglary. If you leave the garage door closed but not locked, he can get inside and again either burglarize the garage or have plenty of time and privacy to work on your side door. He can also hide inside the garage and shout "Surprise!" when you drive in.

The open garage door is not the only way the would-be burglar can see if your car is at home. Any window opening to the garage serves the same purpose for him. These windows should be covered with a plastic material that will let in light but not sight, or the glass should be frosted.

Another invitation to the housebreaker is the note on the door. "Macy's—leave package on the porch"; "Timmie—I will be home at 5:30. Go to Oswald's house to play 'til I get home"; "Mabel—meet me at Fran's." A burglar likes nothing better than to know these things. He is far more interested than Macy's, Timmie, or Mabel! I know you have to notify people sometimes. But phone the school and have Timmie notified there. Phone and tell Macy's not to deliver today, or if they're already en route, let them make their own decision. Better a couple of day's delay in receiving your package than a stripped house. And if there is an absolute *need* to notify Mabel, at least tell her to take the note with her.

A hidden doorway is a burglar's dream. He can happily work away at prying your door open without any neighbors or passing police patrol cars seeing him. He has the opportunity of spending enough time to take care of even a strong and well-locked door. Even worse, he can lie in wait for you as you come home. You can't see him soon enough to safely back off, and he can take care of you without anyone witnessing his actions. Even your scream might not help, because no one would know where it came from. Also, if someone is at your door and talking to you, he can force his way in without being seen. Be sure to keep the doorway visible. Don't allow shrubbery, however pretty, to grow up too high and obscure the view. The same thing applies to a window hidden by shrubbery. Clear it out.

Home Alert Program

A good idea is to organize a neighborhood "vigilance" committee. Your local police or sheriff's department probably has an organized program called "Home Alert" or something similar that they will be happy to explain to you and assist the neighborhood in setting up. The results have been fabulous. I have met with my immediate neighbors on either side and across the street, and we have all agreed to keep an eye on one another's homes, watching for strangers hanging around cars cruising the neighborhood (another favorite trick of the burglar on the prowl), and any other suspicious circumstances. A great preventive stunt when you see an occupied parked car that apparently doesn't belong there is to stand on your porch and stare at it for a moment. I like to very obviously jot down the license number. If the occupants of the car are up to no good, they know that they have been spotted and that a witness exists, so they go bye-bye. I can't prove that our neighborhood arrangement has done any good, but none of us has been burglarized. Many others in the general area have been.

Among my readers will be many who hide a key for one reason or another. Most of those keys I could locate in about two minutes. They will be under the mat (a clever place!), above the door, or hanging on a nail behind a plant or somewhere else that isn't immediately visible at the door. But one thing is sure—it will be somewhere very close to the door. I know it. Burglars know it also; they are the ones who told me about it. If you must hide a key, hide it away from the door. Bury it in a waterproof bag or tin in the back yard or planter box. The best places have the look of permanent parts of the house: Tape the key to a wall and lightly nail a piece of molding over it. You only need the key when you've forgotten your own, which shouldn't be too often, and it's easy enough to pull the wood off and use the key. Use your ingenuity. To test your cleverness, have a smart friend try to locate the key after you've hidden it.

Operation Identification. One spectacularly successful technique is "Operation Identification," now being implemented in most cities, usually sponsored by the local police or sheriff's department. They lend you an electric engraving tool, and you engrave your *driver's license* (not car license) *number* on every valuable item you own—the TV set, radio, camera, binoculars, car radio, tape deck, hubcaps, musical instruments, tools—anything that a burglar might conceivably take. Then the law-enforcement agency gives you some decals to be placed at strategic locations around your house and on your car that announce to the world that the property within has been so marked (Figure 3–1). The decals are placed near all logical points of entry, so they can't be missed. The rate of burglaries on premises so marked has fallen off so dramatically that you can't afford not to use it. Just a couple of statistics to convince you: In one small city that had been averaging 56 burglaries a month, the burglaries dropped to exactly *seven* cases in two *years.* In another survey, out of 1,000 homes so marked, none was hit during the first year. During the second year, one was hit, but all the property was recovered. Nationally, the statistics are just about that spectacular. It is cheaper and far more satisfactory than homeowner's insurance (which you should nonetheless keep). The reason it works is that burglars don't steal things with the intention of keeping them; they sell them

FIGURE 3–1.

OPERATION IDENTIFICATION

HAYWARD
POLICE

WARNING!
ALL ITEMS OF VALUE ON THESE PREMISES
HAVE BEEN MARKED FOR POSITIVE IDENTIFICATION
BY LAW ENFORCEMENT AGENCIES
SPONSORED BY HAYWARD CHAMBER OF COMMERCE

to "fences," underworld characters who buy stolen goods at about 10 percent of its value. A fence won't touch items so marked because they can be traced immediately to a burglary and he is in obvious possession of stolen goods. The burglar knows he cannot dispose of items so marked, so what good are they to him? Also, if he is stopped by the police, he is tied directly to a burglary. (Incidentally, we use the driver's license rather than your Social Security number because by law the Social Security number cannot be checked, but a driver's license can.) Call your local law-enforcement agency. Most of them have brochures explaining Operation Identification, and some even arrange to have someone come and mark the items for you.

Night lights

One of the most effective preventive techniques is the use of lights at night. Criminals like to work in the dark, and lights are something they hate and avoid. We use the lights in two ways. The first is to light up the outside of the premises so that anyone attempting to break in or prowling around is visible to the householder, neighbors, or passing police patrol car. A burglar will normally go to the back of the house to do his breaking in, so be sure that you have lights out there. The very least you should have on is the front-porch, back-door, and side-door lights. The common error is to turn them off when you go to bed. No, no, no, no! Leave them on all night. The cost is tiny; the protection is great. One little burglary in your garage with the loss of one bicycle would cost you more than that part of your electricity bill for the next ten years. And ask any rape or assault victim what she would pay to have had it not happen!

The second use of lights is on the inside of the house, primarily to indicate to the burglar that someone is home. Most burglars won't attack an occupied dwelling because the risk is too great. Here's a word of caution. One little table lamp left on in the front room or hall merely advertises to the burglar that it is a nightlight and nobody is home. Drive around your neighborhood and you will be able to spot the houses in which nobody is home. They will be dark or have that one light on.

Most of you do just that, don't you? Instead, be smart. How does your house look when you are home at night? TV or radio on? Several rooms have lights on? Bathroom light on? Probably that little table lamp in the front room is the only light that isn't on! When you go out, duplicate this scene. A radio playing is a pretty good indication to the prowler that someone is home and awake. A television set is much better. If a burglar peeks in and sees a TV on, he knows that someone is home. Leave one or the other on. Leave an upstairs bathroom light on. Leave several lights on around the house. This is very cheap insurance. Electric timers are very reasonable. Attach them to lamps and radios in various rooms in the home so that they go on and off at staggered times.

Keeping a light on all night in an unused bedroom or in your bathroom even when you are home is a good idea, as it not only indicates that someone *is* home, but also that someone is awake. Don't forget that although you leave the house in daylight, you may be coming home after dark. For some reason there seems to be a peculiar reluctance to turn on these safety lights in the daytime, although it is regular procedure when leaving after dark. Turn them on! (Here is where the electric timer is handy.)

Check the security of your lighting system. Many homes have the main circuit-breaker switch somewhere on the outside of the house so that anyone can come along, pull the main switch, and extinguish not only all your outside lighting, but the inside lighting also. Have it safely padlocked so that no one—kids, practical-joking friends, or bad guys—can get at it.

The chances that your house will be chosen as a likely target by a burglar if you lock up, light up, and use the decals are pretty remote. Add a dog to the above, and you're all set!

Door security

Now let's talk about the security of your doors. Door security to most people means the locks on their doors. Actually, we have to first look at the door itself. If it is a weak door to start with, or is partially rotted, or badly hung so that there is a lot of space between it and the doorjamb, (doorpost) or the hinge pins are on the outside, or the doorjamb itself is rotted or weak, the best lock in the world will not make it secure. And this applies not only to the front door, but also to any door that gives access to the house. Side or back doors that have thin-glass upper portions offer no protection either. Builders are currently installing hollow-core doors, because they are cheaper. These consist of little more than a framework covered by thin veneer and can be cut into with pocket knife or broken through with anything from a foot or fist to ordinary tools. Often front doors are paneled, with the panels being thin and poorly set. Again, they can be kicked in and the door unlocked from the inside. Watch out for loose or rotting molding by the doorjamb, which can be pulled away, exposing the locking mechanism. In short, be sure you start with a solid door in the first place. Keep these facts in mind when you are going to build a house. Be sure you specify all the safety features we are going to discuss. It is very cheap insurance, both for your property and for you and your children. If you are moving into a tract home, particularly if it is not yet completed, have the builder replace the inadequate doors and hardware with better-quality materials. The same can be done before you move into the completed house.

Now we'll get to the subject of locks. To start with, unless the original owner specified to the contractor that he wanted secure locks, you probably don't have them. Most door locks can be easily opened by even an amateur burglar with a piece of plastic or a knife faster than you could open it with a key. This book will not go into the complexities of locks, nor will it tell you which one is best for you. Any licensed locksmith can answer your questions and supply and install adequate hardware for you. Many hardware stores now have displays of locks for you to examine. Many law-enforcement agencies give demonstrations on locks; some even offer a service with which an officer or reserve officer knowledgeable in the field will come and survey your situation.

Suffice to say that the most common lock installed in residential construction is the cylindrical, or key-in-the-knob, lock. They are cheap, easy to install, easy to re-key—and lousy. They offer little security; they can be slipped by a piece of plastic or a knife or can be simply wrenched off. Be sure it at least has a deadlatch or trigger bolt to prevent it from being slipped. This is the little steel pin alongside the beveled latch. For security you should have a deadbolt, either as part of your regular lock or installed as a separate item above your regular lock. These are rectangular steel bolts that should slip into the door jamb at least an inch. If you don't want to change your locks, buy a separate deadbolt, but buy a heavyweight one, not a thin piece of metal that a small boy could bend out of the way.

This brings me to one of my pet hates—the little chain that many of you have on your front door. Here is a chance to try a logical and honest approach to self-defense. See if you can tell why your chain isn't effective. Got it? Let's check your answer: Note the little screws holding the two parts to the door and doorjamb. They're probably about half an inch long and inserted into soft wood. How hard a push would it take to jerk those right out of the doorjamb? If you *really* want to see how safe they are, have someone open your door from the inside to the length of the chain, put your shoulder to the door from the outside, and give it a sharp push. Then pick up the screws off the floor (you can do it—the door is standing open), get into your car, and go down and get a good deadbolt. The directions for installation are on the package. Install it! (By the way, if there is a man of the house, show him this section. He will be interested.)

Actually, my hatred of the little chain on the front door does not extend to heavy-duty ones that are correctly installed. If both sides of the apparatus are fastened deeply into solid wood by long, strong screws, it is a very desirable security item and I recommend it. Be sure you mount them so that you leave only a narrow opening, not quite arm-width, when the door is opened. Why would you need more? If someone reaches through this opening and attempts or actually grabs you, slam the door on his arm or hand and keep doing it until he decides to go and play elsewhere. If slamming the door doesn't work (he may have his foot against it), pick up some heavy object and beat on his fingers, which will prove more painful than the punishment you inflicted on his arm. The heavier the object, the better. Then, when he does take off, call the police immediately.

Going back to doors: Did you ever notice that the front door is the one with the heaviest and best lock, the bolts and chains, etc? Do you know that few illegal entries are made through the front door? The easiest door to get through is the sliding-glass patio door and the door leading from the side of the house into the garage. So, after we install the deadbolt lock and other locks to the front door, let's look at the others. Everything I said about the front door goes for the door from the side of the house into the garage (not the garage door; that comes later) and the door leading from the garage into the house, or any other outside door. Even if the front door has a deadbolt, the other doors usually don't. Install them. Consider sliding bolts. Do what you did to the front door. It is easy to get past the garage door, especially if it is a two-car garage. (This isn't a course in burglary—just take my word that it is easy). Also, the noise that a burglar makes breaking in through the side door into the garage may not be heard inside the house, so always keep the door from the garage to the house locked and bolted. It is false security to feel that because the garage is locked, the house is secure. Do both.

In regard to the garage door, I think the best thing for your security that has come along in a long while is the automatic garage-door opener. This means that as you are arriving home, without stopping or getting out of your car, you punch a button in your car, have the door open *and the light go on*—a tremendous advantage—drive right in, and, before you leave the security of your locked car (it is locked, isn't it?), punch the button again, which closes the door automatically. The elapsed time is about 20 seconds, hardly enough time for someone to waylay you, even if he was lurking nearby. Plus, there is no lock to be picked. I strongly recommend them.

Now for the sliding glass patio door, probably the weakest link in your system. There are several things to consider. First, the door frame is made of soft metal, and the lock can be easily popped open by the insertion of a heavy screwdriver between the door and the casing. It takes about a second and makes virtually no noise. These doors can be secured in one of two ways, depending upon which way your door is set. If the door is as it should be, sliding *inside* the permanent, fixed glass, you merely lay a board or heavy dowel (a sawed-off broom handle is fine) in the track or channel that the door slides in so that the door cannot be slid along that track. Make the dowel the full length of the track so that it can't be bounced out or fished out by someone getting the door partway open.

If the door slides open on the *outside* of the house, we must use another method. I again refer you to a locksmith or good hardware store. There are many excellent commercial locks and stops that can be affixed to these doors, and you can install them yourself. However, a quick and adequate solution is to bore a one-quarter-inch hole through the metal frame of the stationary door on the side away from the lock. Bore this hole right through both sides of the frame (while the doors are shut, of course) and through the first side of the frame of the sliding door. Now you can slide a bolt right through the stationary door frame and into the first side of the sliding-door frame. The door is pinned in place and can't be opened, nor can the sliding door be lifted off its track and taken out. Make your own security lock or buy one, but do it! As a personal safety precaution, be sure your sliding glass doors are made of tempered glass. This doesn't make them any more burglar-proof, but they won't shatter into killing shards if someone tries to walk through one of them. Mark the glass well with decals at eye level, as it is easy to fail to see the glass and walk through one (I did it).

Windows

As for windows, they are also easy for a burglar to get through. A thin knife can slip the lock on the ordinary double-hung window (where there are two windows, one above the other, and you can raise the bottom one and lower the top one). One way of securing these is to bore a hole right through the top sash of the lower window and halfway into the bottom sash of the top window where they overlap. Then, by inserting a steel pin or a heavy nail through the holes, you have pinned the two windows together and neither can be moved. Sliding windows can be secured as we did the sliding glass doors. If you have louvered windows, there is no good way to secure them. Again, I refer you to the commercial security locks. They are made to fit all kinds of windows.

A popular and very dangerous kind of lock that is sometimes recommended is an inside-keyed deadbolt lock for the doors and windows that can only be opened from the inside with a key. They are very secure from the standpoint that even if someone breaks the glass or cuts a hole through the door, he can't reach in and unlock the window or door. The catch is, in case of emergency, either a fire or prowler, if the key isn't in the lock, you can't get out. Even if the key is in the lock, in a panic situation there is a good chance that you won't be able to open it, and children or guests surely won't. I believe the danger of being trapped inside your house by fire is too great to warrant the use of these locks, and I do not recommend them. Some localities have prohibited their use for this reason.

Another very old idea that is being widely used again is the iron grillwork over doors and windows, particularly in the larger cities. A locked floor-to-ceiling grill at the bottom of inside steps leading to the front door is becoming quite common and provides a lot of security. Grillwork on basement and first-floor windows, some very decorative, is also becoming more common. There are cheaper variations, such as steel bars or wire mesh over windows. There is the same danger here as there is in the inside-keyed lock: How do you get out in an emergency? If the means of exit are blocked off, the cure can be worse than the disease. As a result, some cities have ordinances against their use, mostly because of the danger in case of fire. If you do use either the inside-keyed lock or the grillwork, be sure that there are enough windows and doors that do not have these dangerous impediments to allow you to flee the premises in a hurry.

Another danger point often overlooked by the householder, but not by the burglar, is the window air conditioner. This is set into the window, which, of course, must be partially opened. If the other half of the window is not secured properly, the burglar can merely raise or lower it further and enter. If the air conditioner itself is not properly secured, such as being bolted to the *outside* of the house, the burglar merely has to unbolt it and take it out, and he has a lovely pathway to the inside. Besides, he will add insult to injury and steal the air conditioner as well! Insist that it be installed properly and cannot be removed from the outside and that the other half of the window is secured.

A word of caution to dog and cat owners: The dog and cat doors can also be points of entry for your burglar. Children can often squeeze through (and many of our burglars are children) to burglarize or vandalize your home, or they can be sent through by adult burglars to open the door from the inside. Also, if the doggie-door is in the regular door, the burglar may be able to reach up and unlock the door or use a stick or some other tool to release the locks or catches.

Visibility

With regard to windows, there is another important word on prevention: A woman should never be visible to persons on the outside, particularly if she is alone. Everyone from Peeping Toms to rapists and sadistic killers, let alone normal males, will be attracted if he spots a nude, semi-dressed, or even a fully but enticingly dressed woman through an uncurtained window. Thin curtains will definitely not block anyone's view if there is a light on inside the room. Always draw the blinds (and keep your shadow off it) when dressing or undressing or walking around dressed in provocative clothing. The confessions of many of the rapists and sex deviates contain a statement to the effect "I first saw her through the window. . . ." Don't think you are safe just because you can't see anybody outside or you are on the fourth floor of the apartment house. Peeping Toms (and worse) often use binoculars from nearby hillsides, rooftops, buildings, and other apartments. Then they come to see you. . . . A pulled blind or drape may not be sufficient if there is a crack along the side or bottom through which the prowler could peek. Tonight, run a test of your privacy. Light the lights inside, draw all your drapes and blinds, then go outside and try to peek in. Better yet, get a tall man to do it for you, as he may be more the size of the prowler than you are, and he can spot peepholes that you would miss.

A shield of shrubbery or a high fence is not enough protection either. There are holes in both through which your admirer may peer. Also, suppose, in the darkness, he gets on the inside of said fence or shrubbery? Pull your blinds! If they are Venetian blinds, turn them up, so that if he does peek in he can see only the ceiling. If they're turned down, he may be able to see feet and legs, or at least shadows, and can get a rough idea who, if anyone, is around.

House noises

One of the most common frightening expriences is to hear noises in your home when you are alone in the middle of the night (or, really, at any time). Is there someone in the house? Is there someone prowling around outside or trying to get in? Everybody has been scared silly by this experience at one time or another, although experience has taught us that most of the sou ds are natural and there is really no one there. The real problem is that you have never learned to distinguish the normal night sounds that all houses make from the unnatural noises made by a burglar, prowler, or fire. (Fire makes recognizable noises.) Resolve right now to stop scaring yourself to death unnecessarily, by learning what is normal for your house. Tonight, turn out all the lights (this is part of your conditioning—always try to duplicate the actual stress conditions you would be under in real life), then listen closely for about ten minutes. You can't imagine the collection of sounds you will hear! By *consciously* (there's that word again) listening, you will become aware of noises that you have always heard but turned off as a routine until you were alone and in a position to be frightened. These sounds come from many sources; As the house cools down or heats up, the wood expands and contracts, making all sorts of snapping, groaning, and popping noises; the many electrical circuit-breakers make clicking noises as they turn on and off; the appliances they control (heater, refrigerator, freezer, etc.) start up or shut down; shrubbery rubs against the house; the wind whistles through a hole or crack, or bangs a loose board or shutter; your cat, dog, love bird, or even goldfish, move around or "talk"; even mice, crickets, or other little creatures add their contributions to the din. After you have familiarized yourself with all these sounds, you will no longer be frightened of them, leaving your faculties free to send the alarm when there is a real foreign sound. Besides, isn't the freedom from fear alone worth the effort of learning your house sounds? If you have children or a roommate, have them join you in the experiment. Let them have the same advantages.

Outside prowlers

Next, we'll take up the problem of the burglar or prowler. (You don't know *what* he is, and neither does he—a prowler may start out the evening as a Peeping Tom, see the opportunity for a burglary, surprise a woman inside, and end up as a rapist and murderer.)

If anything drives an experienced policeman wild, it is a scene in a movie or TV play in which a beautiful girl, alone in a house, hears a noise outside or downstairs and, carrying a lantern or flashlight, goes to look. You can tell if there are any policemen in the audience by the grinding of their teeth. Of all the wrong moves, this is one of the worst! You not only place yourself within reach of the prowler, but you may frighten him so that he takes a shot at you, strikes you, or strangles you to keep or stop you from screaming. He may also decide to eliminate a witness. Stay inside and stay out of sight! Don't ever let him know you are a woman and/or that you are alone. If you hear a noise outside the house, don't turn on the inside lights that expose you to view, because he may be peeking through a window (or through your door peephole—did you know they worked both ways?), and he will know just what you didn't want him to know—that you are a woman and apparently alone. He also has the tactical advantage of knowing where you are.

Suppose you feel you should check out the noise first, before you call the police (and you're sure it's outside and not inside); you peek through your peephole, stand to the side of a window and peek out, and tiptoe to the kitchen to peek out the back windows. What have you accomplished? If you actually do see somebody prowling around out there (and the chances are very slim) call the police—how, we'll explain later. But look at what else might happen. You might get there just in time to greet him as he makes his entrance, with the results mentioned above. Or, think about him looking through a window, even if you haven't turned on the lights. As you pass between his eyes and a lighted background, like another window or a light-colored wall, your silhouette will stand out like a shadow picture. One of the surest ways to send him galloping off into the night with the beginnings of an ulcer is to bathe him in light. If you do not have the outside lights on, and you can get to them safely, flip them on. (If necessary, crawl over to the switch.) This puts him in light and also tells him that someone is aware that he is out there and has probably called the police. He'll take his leave from your home and the entire neighborhood. If you can't safely get to the outside-light switches, turn on a couple of inside lights, like that in the bathroom and others that can be seen from the outside, making sure that you, in your nightclothes, don't step into a room and turn on the lights in which the blinds are up, thus making you visible. *If in any doubt at all,* call the police. They know that most of the prowler calls are unfounded, but they'll never catch the actual prowlers unless they get the calls. Resolve all doubts in favor of calling. It's really not a good idea to call a neighbor. What do you want him to do? He is untrained, probably doesn't have a weapon, and wouldn't be sure how or if to use it if he had. Besides, you're putting his life in danger. Also, when the police arrive, they'll see a guy wandering around your backyard with a flashlight (your neighbor!). They just got a prowler call about some guy in a backyard . . . . Write your own script from here on. Call the professionals.

Inside prowlers

Now let's say that you hear a prowler inside the house, or in the process of breaking in. If you are in bed, you *should* have your bedroom door locked. If it's not, quietly lock it. Take your phone under the covers with you and dial "operator" (don't try to dial the police number), say, "Police emergency" and your address, and she'll do the rest. This way, if you do get cut off before the police answer, the operator has your address and will notify them, and they'll send units anyway to find out what's wrong. When the police answer, tell them about the prowler and stay on the phone until they tell you to get off. This gives them a link between you and the squad car that's coming to help you and to the police who may be surrounding your house.

There are many other considerations, however. Do you have kids in another room? Do you have a dog with you? (Should you send him out and maybe get him killed?) Is the phone in another room? There is no one who can set up a plan of action that will cover all the many circumstances that might be present. I have one excellent suggestion: Take a good look at your home situation and decide—right now—what you should do under the various conditions that might occur. If you are smart, and you are home, you will put this book down as soon as I say "Now!" and physically go through the actions you would take. I said "*physically* go through the actions," not just think about them. You may find that things are not what you thought they were. The phone cord might not reach as far as you thought. A crucial door may open out instead of in. There may not be a lock on a door where you thought there was. By going through the actions now, you will remember them under stress and are far less likely to panic or do the wrong thing. Okay? *Now!*

Good for you! If you have any kids or anyone else staying in the house, get them to do the same thing, so you have a plan of action worked out. It could save you—and them.

Notice I said to have anyone else in the home do the same thing. It is of vital importance that you have your children and babysitters aware of the same preventive and safety precautions that you follow. If there are kids at home, discuss the necessary techniques with them and have them role play until they are as proficient as you are. The same goes for a roommate. If you take all the precautions and your roommate doesn't, the whole advantage is lost.

I just mentioned dogs. Let's discuss them in regard to your protection. If you are talking about your *personal* protection, little Buttercup, who is as cute as a button—and about the same size—just isn't going to make it as a ferocious killer. Although

Buttercup may regard herself as such, be as brave as two hungry tigers, and loyal to the death, she just plain doesn't have the equipment. For personal protection you need a large dog that can put up competent battle with your assailant. Better yet, the dog should be big enough so that the mere size and evident ferocity will be enough to make the assailant decide that you, notwithstanding your obvious desirability, are just not worth becoming a doggie *hors d'oeuvre* over. The breed doesn't make a great deal of difference. Very few men will attack you in the presence of even a medium-sized dog, let alone one who looks as if he should be equipped with a saddle.

However, if you are talking about *house* protection, so that Buttercup acts like a four-footed audible burglar alarm, she will be quite adequate. The burglar knows barking dogs don't bite—if he doesn't enter the house, which he ordinarily won't. He figures the barking will attract attention, and although he has a pretty good idea as to the size of Buttercup from the size of her bark, he still doesn't relish even a nip on his ankle. Interviews with burglars indicate they stay away from houses with dogs. A dog chained to a tree in the back yard is no danger to the burglar. Let him stay inside and give him the run of the house so that he can personally extend a welcome when the burglar enters.

There are a couple of more points to be made before we leave this subject. Most burglars will run to avoid being caught. Don't get between him and his escape route; he'll bowl you over to get out. If you have no help coming, call to an imaginary male, e.g., "Jim! Call the police!" Then give him time to get clear before you go to your phone. You'll probably hear him take off.

If, however, you are face-to-face with the burglar, and the situation is such that there is nothing you can do, don't panic. If you panic, he probably will too and may take physical action to keep you from running out, stop you from screaming, or just assault you as a mindless reaction to his own panic. Step aside—remember, be sure you are not between him and his escape route—and tell him to take what he wants, that you have no intention of trying to stop him. Try to note his description, physical and clothing, to help in his apprehension later. Note particularly anything unusual about him, such as scars, birthmarks, peculiarities of any kind. They are worth more to a policeman than his height and weight, which you would probably guess wrong anyway. Don't be too obvious about this. Carefully jotting down notes about his description while he is there might make him a wee bit suspicious. But do it as soon as he leaves so you won't forget.

If you wake up and find that the burglar is in your bedroom, your best bet is to pretend to be asleep until you hear him leave. If he hadn't molested you up until then, he probably has no intention of doing so and will complete his burglary and leave. If you do wake up and scream or try to fight him, he may physically assault you to shut you up—and get some other ideas in the process. You are far less provocative while under the bedclothes than you are in a babydoll nightie, so stay under the covers in any event. Don't try anything until you hear him leave. Then lock your bedroom door and call the police. They have a good chance of picking him up in the neighborhood under these circumstances, so don't delay the call.

Another point: If you are coming home and find the house turned inside out, don't rush in to see what was taken; the burglar may still be there. Back off, go to a neighbor's, or drive away and call the police from elsewhere. If you are driving up to your home and something doesn't look right, don't stop. Drive by and see if you can tell what bothered you. If you can't, go to the neighbor's and take it from there. The basic rule is: Don't fool with him—let the police handle it.

Someone at the door

Now let's talk about a different kind of intruder, the one who comes to your door to talk or push his way in. One basic trick many women use routinely when answering the door while alone is to call out to an imaginary male, "I'll get it, Harry," or other words to indicate that some male is on the premises. If the caller turns out to be a friend, simply explain why you did it so they don't think you've gone a little dingy. You can use this same trick with a telephone caller so that they don't think you are alone.

First of all, you should have a peep hole, preferably one

with a wide-angle lens that will pick up anyone who is crouching close to the door or off to the side. (I like to keep a little cap on the inside of mine so that no one can use it to look into the house.) Another good item is a speaker, through which you can talk with someone outside (or downstairs, if you are in an apartment). On a par with the nonthinker who goes outside to see what the noise is, I place the one who can't see anybody through the peep hole, because he's off to the side or has his thumb over it, *so opens the door to find out who's there!* You don't think it happens? It does!. Don't *you* do it. If you can't see who it is or do not recognize the caller, talk to him through the door. If he claims credentials of some kind, have him hold them up to the peep hole. If it's late at night or you're not satisfied with the credentials, no legitimate official or repairman will object to your getting his name and calling the company or department and asking if the credentials are legitimate. If he does object, call the police. If he is legitimate and objects, report him to his company. He is wrong! If you can't get any intelligible or logical conversation out of your caller, or you are suspicious, or he won't go away, call the police. Let them check him out.

If the caller tries to push his way through the partially opened door and you are unable to slam it shut, you can use a heel-of-the-hand blow up under his nose. (We'll teach you this blow later.) If you use it hard enough (with surprise, of course), you may slow him down, force him back, or even send him fleeing, because he is hurt. In any case, it is the best physical defense that can be used in this situation.

Blocking a door

Here is a physical trick to block a door. I call it "the doorstop." The average person tries to hold a door against someone by placing his shoulder against it. If you are standing on anything but a hard, rough-surfaced floor, you will probably lose the shoving match. Or, if the person on the other side is larger, the extra weight will win. You are probably smaller than most men, but you can hold a door against a large man. Place the toes of your right foot (assuming the door handle is on your right) on the door about three inches above the ground and

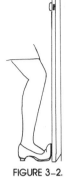
FIGURE 3-2.

about two inches in from the edge. Now, pressing your toes hard against the door, slide your bent toes down the door until the rest of your foot is flat on the floor (Figure 3–2). Keep your weight on your right leg, pushing down hard. This leverage will hold against even a big man's pressure from the other side. Try it!

(Now let's get off to a good start so that the reader and the author understand and appreciate each other. Throughout this book, I, the author, will say "Try it!" To really get the most out of the book, that is exactly what you, the reader, should do—try it. Right then. I say it because it is at that very point that the experience is necessary so that you can go on to the next point and understand it fully. If you will trust me and do it when and where I tell you, you will get the maximum value from my efforts. Trust me. Merely reading it is absolutely no substitute for trying it.)

So, like I said, *try it!* You can even do this barefooted, as the pressure is not against the toes but against the sole of your foot. This trick should be used every time you open your door and don't want to swing it wide to admit someone. Open it a crack to talk, have the door against your "doorstop," and talk around the edge of the door. If your visitor tries a push, you can block it. Immediately try to close the door, using your foot as well as your hands for leverage. Be careful not to take the weight and pressure off your foot, or you will have lost your leverage. A good, strong chain, correctly installed, is a great help here, with your "doorstop" to back it up. Another word of caution: Be sure the chain is in place before you start to open the door. Many people use the chain only when they lock up for the night, or at night when they are suspicious. Use it all the time. Take time to put it on when the doorbell rings. It is excellent insurance.

Entry by pretext

Criminals also try to gain entry to your home under the pretext of an emergency. They'll tell you that there's been an automobile accident, that someone has had a heart attack, or that their car has broken down. They then ask to use your phone to call the ambulance, tow truck or whatever. As soon as you let them in, you've been had. This type of entry has been appearing more and more often on police records. The latest refinements have a woman, often carrying a baby, making the plea. Sometimes it is a request for some water for the baby or to use the bathroom. The answer, of course, must be "No." In recent cases the woman has been accompanied by a man who is out of sight and pushed through as soon as she got the door open. If a call to an ambulance, tow truck, or the police is necessary, offer to make it for them, shut the door, and then make it. If they lose interest and tell you "never mind" when you offer to make the call, make the call anyway—to the police. They'll be very interested in locating and talking to your visitors. Don't think that you can distinguish between the legitimate and illegitimate requests, because the people who work these rackets sound more plausible than the legitimate people.

Forced entry

If you have refused admittance to someone who then tries to break the door down, don't stand there and try to hold the door. Leave immediately for a healthier climate, but do it quietly. Don't give your position away. If he thinks you're going elsewhere, he'll try to intercept you. Keep him occupied breaking down your door. *The basic rule is:* Don't run upstairs or somewhere else where you are in a dead end and he can trap you, like into a bathroom without a window or other exit. Run— quietly!—to the back door and out, if there is a neighbor to go to—but not if your backyard is securely fenced in and you would be trapped again (of course, you may be safer there in view of the neighbors than in your house). Maybe your best bet would be to get to your garage and into your car. At this point, you should make a resolve to always know where your car keys are. The smart ones keep an extra key available in the house in case they lose the regular key or lock it inside the car. Is this a real emergency? Don't play according to rules, then. Don't try to open the garage doors, unless you have an automatic opener. First be sure you're locked inside your car, with all buttons down and windows up. Then start your car and take off—if you have to, right through the closed garage door. If worst comes to worst, and you can't break out, stay in your car, lean on the horn, and keep trying to drive somewhere. If you are halfway out of your garage with a busted door blocking you, the neighbors should show some curiosity and call the police. If you want to make sure, lower your window no more than an inch and keep hollering *"Police!"* Noisy and dramatic, but a lot better than being trapped in your upstairs bedroom by a rapist (or worse)! If you can't get out or to the garage, retreat deeper into the house, locking doors behind you, preferably heading for a room with a phone. Pretend you have the police on the phone, even if there is no phone there. He doesn't know that there isn't and can't afford to stay around to be part of the welcoming committee. Don't neglect the opportunity to lean out a window and scream for help. If you've got all your wits about you and the prowler can hear you, try something like "Hurry up, Spike, he's in the house now!" I'll bet he won't be for long!

If he does break down the front door while you are still there, your nearest exit may be the same door. Use surprise and speed, in combination with one of the personal weapons or other techniques we'll be working on later, and get to the outside. Your screams should alert the neighbors to the fact that something unusual is happening. If you have gotten together with your neighbors as suggested earlier, they will take some action. See how it all fits together?

Another wrong move is when the woman, now outside the door, turns and tries to talk to the guy. *Don't!* You're free. Keep going until you either get to help or get it on its way. Otherwise, he may clobber you and drag you back into the house. It is surprising and disheartening to see how many times women break free and then walk right back into the spider's web.

Suppose he does get in and does not immediately assault you. Take a quick assessment of the situation, and if you're not in a good defensive position, it might be better to pretend to go along with him. Don't go directly from frightened hysteria to seductive harem girl with fluttering eyelashes; even a real dummy would be able to see a trick coming up. Show resignation to the situation, or whatever you think best under the circumstances and play it by ear until your opportunity comes along. What have you got to lose? Try something right away and you're probably a goner. Talk! Pretend your husband is coming home. Promise! Offer him a drink. (Don't try to get him drunk—that happens only in the movies, when he finally passes out and the girl escapes, usually with the secret papers.) Maneuver toward the door or other exit. Go to the bathroom and out the window if it is feasible. Can you get to your phone without him knowing and starting the rough stuff? How would you flee your house if a fire blocked the door? (You should already know and have practiced this.) You might use the same method. Again, play act these things now. You will be surprised what you will learn and how a little practice will teach you to keep your head.

Use available weapons

Let's say this is a situation in which you have to resort to physical force for self-defense. You are in your home, where you know the location of everything. Your personal (natural) weapons are great, but maybe you'd better use some harder objects from your household supplies. He will definitely notice the difference between your untrained fist and a large glass ashtray across his nose. Use a heavy object to hit him with, like a poker, vase, ashtray, iron frying pan, baseball bat, or whatever you have handy. A lamp is lousy, because it is tied down with a cord. If you use lightweight objects, he'll just cover up and keep coming. You need something heavy enough to hurt him. Use any hot liquid from the stove—hot, not warm—or a hot pan. Household liquids like ammonia, toilet-bowl cleaner, or alcohol, when thrown at his eyes, will give you a chance to escape. Pepper is excellent. Pour it into your hands first. How about a knife? Probably not, unless you know how to use it. Most knives are too small and light to be effective anyway; you don't have enough power to cause it to penetrate, and it means you have to get within his reach. If the emergency is severe enough to warrant the use of lethal force, an ice pick would be a logical weapon, because not as much strength is needed for penetration. If you have to use it, conceal it until the last minute and thrust without preliminary motions—no roundhouse or over-the-head motions. The danger here is that he may take the knife or ice pick away and use it on *you*.

When I say *"Now!"* put the book down and look over your house. See what would be effective to use. Role play. You'll find you'll do a lot of things wrong and spot the errors yourself. This means you won't make those errors if the situation becomes real. This is your practice. Make the most of it. *Now!*

CHAPTER FOUR

APARTMENT SECURITY AND DEFENSE

Although the safety problems of the homeowner and the apartment house dweller are identical in most respects, there are some differences that should be pointed out. It would appear that apartment living would be safer, because many people share the same building, furnishing safety in numbers. Unfortunately, it doesn't always work out that way. Particularly in big cities, apartment dwellers tend to withdraw into their apartments, shutting out the problems of their neighbors. Also, you do not have control over part of your environment, such as the garage, lobby, hallways, elevator, gardens, and so on. This responsibility is shared not only with all the other tenants, but also with the landlord, superintendent, or custodian, who may not be on the premises all the time. This, in turn, means that you cannot set up that environment as you would like for safety, an advantage the homeowner has.

You do have something of a choice in the selection of your apartment. By choosing a low-crime neighborhood and a building that offers such safety features as well-lighted and visible garages, doorways, lobbies, and hallways, good locks, and an interested and alert owner or manager, you can eliminate a great many dangers. The same rules set out under "Home Security and Defense" apply in equal measure in apartment living, with a few additions.

Garage area

Let's start with the garage. In many cases, these are cavernous areas, poorly lighted and usually deserted, and often some distance from the entrance (and relative safety) of the building. Often they are open to anyone who cares to wander in and lie in wait. There is no easy remedy to this situation, except to try to get the landlord to install adequate lighting. If you can, obtain the parking place closest to the entry door, possibly by arranging a trade with some male who isn't too frightened of being assaulted. When arriving at the garage, use the same ground rules of watching for loiterers or unauthorized people in the area; if they are there, don't enter. Drive away until they are gone, or arrange for some one to meet you. This arrangement should be worked out in advance with other tenants. If you do drive in and discover some danger, drive out again, or if you are blocked off, remain in your locked car, leaning on the horn and keeping your lights on. The horn should scare off any would-be attacker and will also attract help, if only someone who objects to the noise. A pattern of horn blasts can be worked out with other tenants as a signal so that they will personally respond when they hear the signal or will call the manager or police. Remember—these signals must be set up in advance and with responsible people who will take it seriously. When you do arrive in the garage, before you unlock or get out of the car, get your apartment key out of your purse and into your hand. If it is on a ring of keys, select the correct one and have that specific key in your hand. Do not delay; enter the building immediately. Again, the less time taken, the less opportunity an attacker has.

Lobby area

If you reach the front door leading to the lobby and there is someone else there, do not let him in with you unless you know him to be a tenant or someone who has a right to be there. Let him use his own key or push the buzzer so that the person he's visiting can let him in. It may be embarrassing to shut the door in his face, but safety is not always easy. Remember your assertiveness training.

If you are at the outside door and are accosted, try to push as many apartment buttons as possible and scream and carry on as loudly as you can. The other tenants will turn on their intercoms to find out what is going on and will hear your screams. The voices coming out of the speaker saying "Who is it? What's wrong?" will scare off the attacker, as he knows that someone, whether a tenant or the police, will be there shortly. If you are grabbed and can't reach out to push the buttons, try to lean or fall against them. The more buttons you push and the longer you lean on them, the more action you will get.

The next logical danger point is the automatic elevator, a source of many problems. We will handle the elevator in a separate chapter, because the problem of the elevator also applies to situations other than apartment houses.

Internal security

One of your main concerns is the security of your apartment door. Before you even move in, have the locks changed. The former tenants, in fact, maybe several sets of former tenants, might have retained keys, and you have no idea how many friends of the former tenants had been given keys and not returned them. Any of these could walk in on you at any time. And if you're changing the locks, why not upgrade them at the same time?

The superintendent will have a key to your apartment, but he has no unrestricted right to enter at any time. Check your lease or rental agreement for the rules, and never, never allow him to barge in whenever he feels like it, whether you are home or not.

The internal security of your apartment should be handled just as it would be in the private home. Even if your landlord has not provided safety chains, peep holes, or special locks for your sliding doors, ask for them, and if necessary, provide them yourself. I will again remind you that living on the upper floor may not prevent someone from coming through your window or patio from a fire escape, adjoining patio, or some other means.

If someone pushes your buzzer from the front door, do not—I repeat, *do not*—push the door-opening button unless you know who it is. This is the usual way unauthorized persons get into the hallways of apartment houses. They may be peddlers or burglars, who can usually find some unthinking tenant who will push the buzzer and let them in. If you do see someone wandering the hallways or if a peddler appears at your apartment door, immediately call the superintendent so that the unauthorized visitor can be escorted out. The rapist, burglar, or robber often turns out to be a peddler who saw an opportunity or who uses the peddler cover to gain entry and as an alibi if caught.

There will be many times when you will leave your apartment temporarily: to visit a neighbor, put out the garbage, go for the mail, go to the laundry room, or for many other reasons. *Never* leave your door open or unlocked. In the few moments you are gone, someone, even an amorous neighbor, could slip in and present you with a completely unpleasant problem upon your return. A good idea is to have an extra key mounted on an elastic bracelet that you keep on a hook or table near the front door, but not visible, because some tradesman or casual visitor might take it and visit you later. When you have to leave on one of these little errands, you simply slip the bracelet on your wrist and won't have to rummage through your purse to find your key. It also means that the key is immediately available should you have to run to the safety of your apartment in a hurry. It is not only a convenience, but will ensure that you will lock your door because it's so easy! Put this book down right now and go get or make a bracelet, put your extra key on it, and put it where you will use it. If you don't have all the necessary items, write a note—right now—to buy them. If you don't, there is an excellent chance that it won't get done, and your safety is just a little diminished. The secret of making this book useful is not just reading, but *doing* the things discussed. I'll wait while you handle this. . . .

These little errands, particularly going out to the garbage can or the laundry room, are usually done at night, and can be dangerous. Whenever possible, schedule such activities for daylight hours. Make taking the garbage out the first thing you do in the morning, rather than the last thing at night. Arrange for a neighbor to do her laundry (or *his* laundry) at the same time. Again, it is usually the lone woman who is attacked.

Although many apartment-house dwellers do not become friendly with their neighbors, it is very advisable to make friends with nearby tenants. It is not necessary to become bosom buddies, but you must make their acquaintance as a necessary start if you are to set up a mutual-assistance pact. You want them to know you so that when you call for help, they will respond. People always respond to cries for help from friends but often ignore the cries from strangers. Set up an arrangement so that you will respond to one another's cries or pounding on the walls, ceilings, or floors, as the case may be. Arrange to call one another's apartments if you hear noises when the person is not supposed to be home, with a follow-up call to the superintendent or the police if there is no answer.

That brings me to the next point. Be sure you have an emergency list of telephone numbers posted near the telephone so you can get help quickly when you need it: the numbers of the neighbor we were just discussing, the superintendent, the fire department, and the police. A duplicate of this list should be by your bedroom phone also, and don't make the mistake many do in having it scribbled, in faint pencil, small letters, and mixed up. Make it large, clear, and easily readable in a dim light, without your glasses. If you now wear an embarrassed smile, immediately go to your illegible list and rewrite it according to the guidelines (then criticize your friends for not being as sensible as you are).

Know where the fire exits and fire escapes are: You may need to escape more than a fire. When you are trying to escape, it is better to be caught by your attacker on an exposed fire escape in full view of a fascinated audience than alone in a deserted hallway. This would be a great time for you to check out those fire escapes. Be sure you know how to open the window (try it!) that leads to the escape ladder. If not, have someone show you. Learn these things now, rather than during an emergency.

CAR
SECURITY
AND DEFENSE

When you really stop to analyze it, your car is one of the safest places you can be. It is a little steel fort with one very unfortlike characteristic—it can run itself and its occupants away from the battle and head for safety. Custer should have had such a fort! So, when discussing car security and defense, we're really talking basically about two dangerous situations: when you're caught outside your car and when someone forces his way into your car.

Preventive steps

We will start this discussion the same way we did the last chapter, with prevention, the easiest form of self-defense. Let's start with the physical condition of the car itself. Do all the doors and windows work? Do the door locks work? If not, you can't lock yourself inside your fort, your main place of safety. Get them fixed! Is your car in good operating condition? Are your tires safe? Do you have enough gas? If not, a mechanical breakdown, flat tire, or empty gas tank can leave you stalled in a dangerous place and expose you to a situation in which you might be attacked. Does your horn work? If not, how can you attract attention and help if you need it? Get your car in top condition. It may avoid the need of using other parts of this book. Stick to well-lighted and well-traveled streets as far as possible. You are safer in general and certainly safer and closer to help should you break down. Some women have taken to wearing men's hats while driving at night. The silhouette is that of a man and therefore of no interest to the attacker. With current hair styles, the deception won't be noticed.

Many assaults on women take place while they are walking to or from their cars. You are the safest when your car is in a

65

locked garage, so use it if you have one. If you do have one and use it in conjunction with an automatic garage-door opener (discussed in detail in the chapter on home security), you have eliminated most of the dangers in going to and from your car at home. For a lone female, this will avoid much of the fear and nervousness of travel at night. If a door-opener is not feasible, a simple precaution is to take no more time than is necessary in opening and closing the garage doors, especially at night. Any loading and unloading of packages, or car housekeeping, should take place in the garage with the doors closed and locked. If your garage is not attached to the house, don't take two or three trips from the garage to the house with packages at night; except for frozen foods, most of the items can wait until morning, and you have exposed yourself that much less. Remember that most victims are targets of opportunity. The chance of someone lying in wait for you to get home is not very likely. Usually he happens to be in the area, sees you alone in the open garage, and takes advantage of his good fortune. The less time you are visible and available to him, the safer you are.

One way to shorten his available time is to have your keys in your hand ready to insert into the lock immediately, without having to fumble in your purse or pocket. This applies to both the car key and the house key, depending upon which you are heading toward. Before you leave the security of the house or car, get the keys in your hand. You have an added bonus here if you want it; those keys are a weapon. Carry them in your closed fist with the sharp edges projecting out (Figure 5–1), with your house key on top so that it is easily available when you reach your door, and the rest projecting from the bottom of your fist. Then, if you are attacked, use the keys in a slashing motion across your assailant's face, or any other exposed flesh if the face is not available. Do not use the method that is usually taught (Figure 5–2), with the keys projecting through the knuckles. Experience shows that when your assailant grabs your fist and squeezes, you will be in severe pain and rendered helpless. Try it and see.

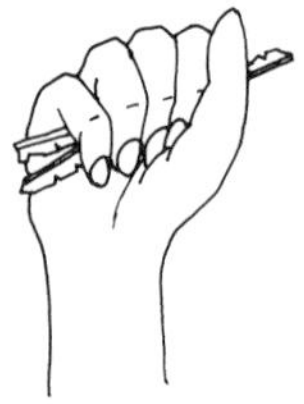

Another simple precaution is when you are approaching your home and see someone loitering in the area or sense any situation that might turn out to be dangerous. Don't stop. Drive on. Go around the block until the person has had a chance to

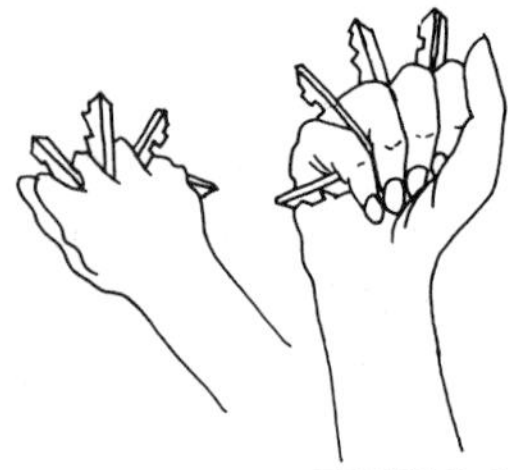

FIGURE 5–1.

FIGURE 5–2.

clear out of the area, and then return. If he is still there, go elsewhere and telephone the police. Let them do the checking out. Not only won't they mind; they'll appreciate it. Preventing crime is their number-one priority.

If you see a strange car parked in your driveway, be especially wary. Even a strange car parked in front of your house when there are many parking spaces elsewhere should at least attract your attention. No, I'm not suggesting that you call the police when you see the car in front of your house; it is just that this is the type of early warning that gives you a chance to back off before you walk into danger. So that you can better understand this, let's check the reasoning. Ordinarily, people park as close to their destination as they can. In a residential neighborhood, you would park in front of the house you are visiting, wouldn't you? Certainly you would never park in someone else's driveway! Therefore, these cars are an out-of-the-ordinary pattern. There are many reasons for their being there legitimately: The driver parked on his side of the street and walked across the street to the house he was visiting instead of making a U-turn and parking in front; there were no parking spaces near his destination when he arrived, although there are now; he didn't know the exact location of the address he was seeking and parked in the general area and walked up and down until he located it. All logical, but you don't know if the car's presence is legitimate or not. Simply be alert and watchful for signs of burglary or a prowler. Look sharply at your house—and neighboring houses—for any signs of entry. Look for any articles stacked or piled up outside (a good indication of a burglary). As you enter, be very alert for signs of entry. If you see anything that tends to confirm your suspicions, back off right now and go for whatever help is available or logical under the circumstances. Remember, decide all questions in favor of safety.

One of the common methods used by an attacker is to hide in the back seat of your car when it is parked. This is usually at the supermarket or some other place where you have parked for a short period of time, although it could happen anywhere. The best way to foil him is to keep your car locked whenever you are not in it, even if you are "just running in for a minute." If it is locked, he can't hide in it. Isn't that simple? You'll find that if you make it a habit to lock your car *every time you leave it,* even if it's for a moment, it becomes as natural as shutting the door, and you have eliminated the attacker, and, to a large extent, the car thief. Most car thieves go for unlocked cars, particularly those with the keys in them. In any case, before you enter your car, make it a habit to glance into the back seat area to make sure it is clear. If you *do* see someone hiding, don't scream and alert him; he's likely to leap out and grab you, if for no other reason than to shut you up. Instead, quietly back off and go to a place of safety and notify the police. Then *they* can leap out and grab *him!*

Your dog, whether it be a fierce, large dog or a lovable little coward, can be a big help. Ordinarily, no one is going to try to enter your car and hide if he is sharing the hiding place with Fido, who would probably tattle on him or try to shred him. The dog will also deter any other kind of entry or assault. Consider whether it is more valuable to leave him home to guard the house or ride with you to guard you and the car.

Driving

Now for the actual driving of your car. Remember that it is your fort. Don't leave the gates of the fort open for the bad guys. When you get into your car, *immediately* lock all your doors and roll up all the windows. Make this a habit *before* you even put the key in the ignition. If you are the only one driving your car, you'll find this usually means just locking the driver's door, because the others are already locked and the windows up. If you have an air-conditioned car, you can always drive around with the windows closed. If not, and you are in hot weather, you can't go around with all the windows up. The trick here is to have them rolled up as far as you can with comfort (and remember to give Fido some air if you're leaving him in the car).

One of the methods of entry used by attackers is to approach your car when it is stopped at a stop sign, stopped in traffic, just as you park, or as you are starting it. He may open the far door and simply slide in beside you, often with a knife, gun, or other weapon, and order you to drive somewhere. He may approach the driver's side, open the door, shove you over or display a weapon, and drive you away himself. If your car is locked and the windows are up, he's not going to be able to get to you unless you panic and open a door. If your windows are rolled down, however, he can reach in and open the door or grab you and make you open the door. The partially rolled-up window makes this more difficult for him. A good general rule when you can't keep the windows rolled up, as in hot weather, is to keep them up until you are moving at a fair speed, then lower the driver's window, moving it up again when you have to stop. This is not much more trouble than putting on your brake.

Parking

When parking, the rules are simple. Whenever possible, park where there are people. An isolated area, such as an alley, a deserted street, an overgrown area with heavy bushes or shrubbery, or an unlighted area, can be dangerous, because you can be taken without anyone witnessing the attack. These areas are very dangerous at night. Check to see if there are any people loitering around, and if so, don't get out of your car until they have left. If they don't leave or if they look as if they had an interest in you, drive away. The loss of a parking space is nothing compared with what you could lose.

At night, try to park under a light or by lighted store windows, (remember, a lighted store window at 8:00 P.M. may not be lighted at midnight after the store closes). In a downtown district where there are public garages, it is far safer to use them than to park several blocks away on the street in a more dangerous area, a poor economy for lone women. A word of warning here: Don't have your house keys and car keys on the same ring. In the first place, if you lose one set, you've lost both sets. But the main security reason is that when you park your car in a public garage, the attendant (who is often transient help) or some outsider who sneaks into the garage can obtain your house key from the ring. It is very simple for him to obtain your address from things in the car, like your registration certificate in the glove compartment. From there he either has a duplicate key made and returns your key or goes directly to your house and burglarizes it. After all, he knows where you are! If he is smart, he will take your car keys as well; then he knows you can't get home for a while, because you are trying to find a locksmith to make a duplicate key for you. Now he has a lot of time to work! He can also wait and visit when you are home, maybe several days later. If he does burglarize your home, don't think that that is the end of it. He still has the key and can pay a return visit at some later date. Have the locks changed immediately.

Consider using a taxi at night. Sometimes, when the cost of parking is considered, it isn't as expensive as you think, and it gives you door-to-door service and safety. If two to five women are going somewhere, it's a good idea to meet at someone's house and go in a taxi, splitting the expense. Do the same thing coming home. Whenever you leave a taxi, have the driver wait until you are safely inside.

Another parking trick when there are two or more women, each with a car, is detailed in the chapter on preventive techniques. They walk to the nearest parked car, and that driver takes the rest to their cars, waiting until they each get started and away. The sensible thing, of course, is to have a car pool, so that there is only one car involved, with a far better chance of parking close and protecting the group. Statistics show that it is the lone woman who is attacked, rarely a group.

When you do get to your car, don't dally. Get in and lock up. Packages can be stowed, coats folded, purse checked, and so on, *after* you are in and locked up. Small packages can be taken in with you at night so that you are not exposed longer while you open the trunk and stow them. Don't enter the car from the passenger's side to stow away your packages; it takes longer and leaves you exposed that much longer. Instead, enter from the driver's side and take the packages in with you. You are also closer to the horn if you need to lean on it. (This is a good time to find out if your horn works without the key in the ignition. Go out to the garage and check. I'll wait.) When you do get into the car, don't leave your purse or package on the seat or your lap where it is visible and can be easily reached by someone from the outside if any window is down.

Some of these problems can be eliminated when shopping at the supermarket at night if you can get the bagger (usually a male) to carry your packages to the car. Do so when feasible, and don't be reluctant to tell the clerk you are afraid. Have him stow the packages, not just leave you there. If this isn't feasible, try to park close to the store so that you are visible from inside. If necessary, wait for the right parking spot to open up. People don't stay in the store indefinitely, and the wait is a small price to pay for safety.

The stalled car

One of the nightmares women have pertains to the stalled car at night, particularly on the freeway. There are no all-inclusive answers to this frightening situation, but common sense will help a lot. First, remember what we said about keeping your car in good condition. A great many times when your car stalls, you had prior warning that it was acting up. That's when it should have been handled! Or a flat tire—when you knew it was getting bald weeks ago. *Now* the preventive techniques make sense to you, but too late. However, if you do have a flat, it often makes good sense to drive slowly to a place of safety: a telephone, a service station, or home. (It is perfectly safe if you drive slowly.) Sure, it may ruin the tire, but isn't it better than sitting on a freeway at night or on a dark street in the wrong part of town? Besides, the modern tire that goes flat is usually about ready for replacement anyway.

But now you are stalled on the freeway. One of the most comforting thoughts you now have is that you bought an auto-club policy of some kind and can get help to change the tire, start your car, or tow it to a garage. I regard this as indispensible to a woman, married or not, because your husband or a male friend may not be stuck on the freeway with you. Help from an expert is far superior to that of an amateur who may stop to help—if that is why he stopped . . . .

The universal signal of highway distress is to raise the hood of your car. This signals passing motorists, who may stop or notify the highway patrol or police for you. If you are a member of an auto club, you may have a little flag you hang on your antenna, so that the passing drivers can notify the auto club, who will send a tow truck to the scene. The raised hood will also stop any passing police unit. In addition to raising the hood of your car and unlocking or raising the trunk lid, turn on the dome light so passing motorists can see that someone is in the car and really needs help, and also turn on your four-way flashers. The flashers not only attract attention to your car; they will also be a big help in preventing someone from plowing into the rear end. You can also have the inside of your hood or trunk lids treated with reflecting material to catch the headlights of cars. Every little bit helps! Tie a handkerchief or piece of white cloth to the door handle or antenna on the traffic side. Be sure you do unto others: Do you notify the police when you see a stalled motorist on the road? Why not? Don't you expect someone to do it for you if you are stalled? The usual excuse is, "Oh, somebody has probably already called the police." If every passerby said that, the stalled car would be there forever. Pull off and call. If it has already been reported, so what? Do unto others. . . .

If you have a flat and somebody stops to help, what do you do? At night, it is best to stay in your car, all locked up, with the window down just enough to talk through, like an inch and a half. When you raised your hood, you should also have unlocked your trunk lid, because now your good Samaritan can get to your spare tire and tools without your having to get out of your secure little fort or hand him your keys, with which he could unlock your fort. If he gets a little irked about your not trusting him, explain that you are scared. Cry—fake it if you have to—it may bring out the male protective instinct again. Remember, if he does want to get at you, his being irked could be a trick to make you feel foolish and come out. If he gets mad and stomps off, your good Samaritan probably wasn't so good after all. Your best bet, if your car is stalled, is to stay in the car and have help brought to you. Don't accept a ride or get out of your car unless you are pretty sure of whoever stopped. Usually a family with a couple of kids or middle-aged women would be safe, but unless you are in physical danger, as you would be on a freeway at night with not enough room to pull your car off the road, you might be better off in the car. Usually a truck driver for a well-known commercial long-haul trucking firm can better be trusted than the plain motorist.

If your car is, or might be, a road hazard, be sure to set out flares. Note: The average motorist who has to light a flare usually has never tried it before, and now, in an emergency, he has to. It is too dark to read the instructions, or he is too excited, or there is no time, or all three, and he doesn't get it lit. I have actually seen a young rookie policeman try to light one with a match! You can buy an extra flare for less than it costs to buy a pack of cigarettes or a cocktail. Splurge! Light one for practice so you'll know how. The instructions are printed right on the flare. Be careful—they drip molten sulphur, which can burn you, so hold them away from you and out like a flashlight so they don't drip on you. If you hold them up like a candle, you will shortly see what I mean. (We'll use this dripping flare for something else later.) Always keep at least one flare in your glove compartment (there is a small size that will fit) or in a holder in the driver's area. If you keep them all in the trunk, you may have to stand in the middle of the freeway with your back to traffic trying to open your trunk to get the flares, not the safest position to be in. Also, in case of accident, your trunk may be jammed. If they are in the glove compartment, you can grab one and exit the car, running down the shoulder of the road while lighting it. Also, keep a two- or three-cell metal flashlight in a holder by the steering column (which is much better than in the glove compartment). This can be a lifesaver by keeping you from being struck by oncoming cars if you have to leave your car, and it can be used as an excellent self-defense weapon. Be sure you check the batteries regularly. They die pretty quickly, even without use.

CB radio

A relatively new fad that is a blessing to the motorist in trouble is the citizen's band (CB) radio, which is now an accessory in many cars. The CBer has immediate contact with the outside world at all times. Day or night, there are always people listening, and not only the amateurs; many highway patrols now have them as standard equipment and will respond to any pleas for help. The obvious practical use for a CB radio is when you have a breakdown, especially if it's on the freeway. You can get help without ever leaving that little fort of a car. It will be even more important when you are being menaced while driving (if someone is following you or trying to play tag or pull you over). You can try to get in touch with the police directly or by relay through some other CBer and arrange for the police to intercept you en route, a delightful surprise for your would-be playmate. I doubt if it will go this far, however, because when he sees you using a microphone, he will probably call time out and leave the area. It will help if you are obviously watching him while you are calling. Whether it is a breakdown or an attack, be sure you furnish accurate location information so that help can get to you.

If you don't have a CB radio, a little subterfuge can be used to accomplish the same results. Pick up anything that resembles a mike (he is some distance away and couldn't possibly tell a fake) and talk into it. An automatic garage-door opener remote-control box looks exactly like a mike; so does an eyeglass case or a pack of cigarettes. I have used this trick successfully on two occasions.

If you are stalled and anyone outside your car is giving you a bad time, the use of the radio will undoubtedly discourage him. Use it quickly, though, because you want help as soon as possible, and an alert bad guy might tear off your outside antenna, blocking your transmission and reception. If he is peering in the windows, smile and nod at him while you are talking on the mike, as if help were on the way. Don't ever scream in panic at the mike—he will know immediately that you haven't reached anyone yet.

Unfortunately, I have to give a word of warning here. There are bad guys as well as good guys with CB radios, and that may be whom you'll attract. There have been instances in which one of these characters has heard the motorist in trouble and been the first on the scene. If so, use the radio again.

If you drive someone else's car and don't know how to operate the CB radio, have someone teach you so that you can use it in an emergency. Then, if you are alone, or the operator is stricken with a heart attack, or is hurt in an accident, you will have the necessary knowledge.

Escape techniques

Now let's get on with the actual physical defenses if you are attacked. If you are locked in and someone tries to get in, *drive off!* If he tries to hang on, it won't be for long. *Don't worry about him!* (Remember Barthol's Law!) On the rare occasion when he stands in front of your car to prevent your driving off, put the car in low gear and drive slowly ahead. He can't possibly stop the car, and he'll eventually have to get out of the way as you slowly pick up speed. *Don't worry about him!* That's his gimmick to bluff you into surrender, panic, or trying to get out of the car to escape (he'll love that!). If there are several troublemakers and they start to rock the car, drive off. By putting your car in the lowest gear, you have maximum power and are least likely to stall your engine. If they lift the rear wheels off the ground (and a crowd can do it) so you have no traction to move, keep gunning the engine. The torque will make them let go and you'll be clear. Drive off to the nearest help. Keep your horn blaring to attract attention. Don't use one long blast; people will think it is a stuck horn and pay little attention. Instead, in an emergency, when you want all the attention you can get, use short blasts.

If the bad guys are following you down the highway, keep to the far-left lanes so that you can't be forced off to the right side of the road. Note that you can't see what's going on in a car parked off the right side of the road, and by the same token, no one would see you if *you* had been the one forced off the right side of the road and were in danger. A car off on the left side, however, is a traffic hazard, is observed by each passing motorist, and the attackers have little room to maneuver. Besides, your attacker is in danger from traffic if he is trying to get into your car.

Now suppose you are stopped. You forgot to lock your car door and someone opens it and slides in. *Don't wait*—slide right out the other side and don't look back. Run for help immediately. Let them know you're coming! Scream your head off. Your sudden exit and flight will probably take your visitor by surprise, and if help is anywhere near, he'll probably be taking off in the other direction, possibly in your car if you didn't grab the keys as you exited. If you can take the keys, do so. It denies him the use of a car and he'll be more easily caught. Besides, he can't use it to chase you. If he does catch you, he can't drive you off into the hills somewhere. If he enters your car and you *can't* get out, grab the keys and throw them as far away as you can, preferably in bushes or high weeds, or somewhere else where he can't easily find them. Now what's he going to do? He usually can't attack you there and he can't drive off with you (which is almost always his intention), so he has to take off on foot, mumbling to himself, while you think of all the terrible physical punishment you could have inflicted on him if you had only thought of the personal weapons in time. . . . If you do have to struggle, use the methods taught later in this book, lean on the horn whenever possible, and scream to attract all the attention you can get.

Physical counterattacks

Now let's change the problem: Your car is stalled, you can't drive off, and the guy's trying to break into your car. It is *not* easy to break out the window glass of a car, so you have time to plan a little, *if you don't panic.* (Right here is where you learn how to avoid panic. Read what I say, then think about it. Play act the scene, preferably physically, but at least mentally. Then these thoughts will come back to you in the emergency. I'm not kidding. This is one way to prevent panic.)

Here are some of the things you can do: If he's reaching through the half-opened window, roll it up as tight as you can. It hurts! He'll usually jerk his hand back before you can trap it, but if you do catch it, keep the window wound up as tight as you can, then start working on the trapped arm and hand, after first sliding far enough away so that he can't reach you. If you get the chance, bite as hard as you can. Beat on his fingers, the back of his hand, and wrist with a flashlight or any other heavy object in reach. Stab the same areas with your fingernail file, pin, knife, or whatever. Burn him with the car cigarette lighter, your own lighter, or a match. Do *anything* to hurt him, and don't get chicken! You may be saving your life! After you have hurt him badly enough, ease the window down just enough to let him pull his arm out, but only if you have a chance to drive away. If you can't drive off, your best bet is to leave him there in the trap, and if he is the only attacker, get out the other side and take off. However, be sure he is tightly held.

If he is breaking the glass to get in and you can't drive off, there is little you can do but lean on the horn, scream, and get something heavy ready to use. When he finally knocks out a big enough hole, he has to reach his hand in to unlock the door. That's when you go into action. The red-hot cigarette lighter would work. I prefer a really heavy object, like a metal flashlight, to smash down on his fingers as they come through. A highway flare can be used to hit him with. Remember that he is putting his hand through broken glass. Your blows will force his hand or arm onto the glass. If he's knocked a hole in the window and puts his hand through, roll the window *down* suddenly. That'll trap him and keep him from opening the door. Administer the workout on his arm as detailed above.

If all else fails, remember the highway flare in the glove compartment. Not many people are willing to go up against a lighted flare! The mere threat of lighting it will give him pause. If worst comes to worst, wait until the last moment (it will take a few seconds to light it and get it going) and shove the burning end onto any part of him that is available. It will stop him, and he will be easily identifiable by the police later when you report it. Be careful of your own safety: You can be burned by the dripping sulphur, and it is also a fire hazard, but we are only doing this as a last resort anyway. If you are outside of your car and he is trying to get at you, keep the flare out in front of you and keep flicking the molten-sulphur drippings at him. He'll keep his distance! If he is stupid enough to close in on you, don't hit him with the flare; thrust it at him so he meets the burning end. I guarantee he will recoil.

The last word on car security: If you are in the car and can't drive off, the car is still your fort. Don't panic and try to get out and run. Once you are out of your fort, he has you. Stay there!

CHAPTER SIX

OBTAINING HELP

"Get help!" This is a common instruction given in books and lectures on this subject. The only trouble is, no one tells you where and how. No one can tell you exactly, because the situations in which you need help cover almost every conceivable set of circumstances. The best I can do here is to give you some ideas with the hope that they will trigger your mind to work if the situation ever demands it. Be imaginative. Right now let your mind rove around and see how many methods you can think of to obtain help. Set up situations in your mind. By day. By night. Downtown. On a country road. Late at night. On the freeway . . . . It's the best practice you can get. Whether you know it or not, your mind is being trained, and it may stand you in good stead someday.

The obvious first: Go for a policeman, the one person who isn't going to turn down your plea for help, the one person who is both trained and equipped to handle your problem. You can get a policeman by calling on the phone; by flagging one down on the street; by creating a disturbance, such as screaming, leaning on your horn, or anything that will attract someone else's attention so *he* (or *she*) will call the police.

Screaming

At this point, let's examine screams as to their efficiency in getting help to you. All the books say to scream loud and long when you are being attacked, but under some circumstances, that could be bad advice. The danger always to be considered in screaming is that it may force your assailant into eliminating the source of the screams—namely, *you!* If you are close to people and help, it is likely that the attacker will take off, because he has to. Help will be arriving immediately and he and his activities will be pin-pointed. He is in immediate danger of discovery and capture and has no time to spare to take care of you. If, however, you are *not* close to people, he *has* time to change the situation by shutting you up, with an excellent chance that no one will be able to locate the disturbance. A single scream, not repeated, is all too often shrugged off by those who hear it. After all, if a woman were really in trouble, she'd still be screaming, wouldn't she? People look for logical and face-saving reasons for not getting involved, and the reasons why people hesitate to help are discussed later in this chapter. So screams will attract attention but, sadly, in today's world, may not always bring help. So, when do you and when do you not scream? Only the person involved has the knowledge and the right to make that judgment. Usually the first scream is automatic, but what if there is a knife at your throat? There are many situations in which you might have to remain silent and await a later and better opportunity to scream, run, or counter-attack. There just aren't any simple answers, are there?

However, we *can* set out some general rules. First, a scream that can't be heard is no good at all. Be sure you scream as loudly as you can and for as long as you can. Don't stop! Keep them coming! Remember, a single scream, unless you are visible, will not help much, because it is often impossible to determine its source. Many times police roam an area, trying to find out where a scream came from, but all they have now is silence. Give them something to zero in on. One suggestion: When you are inside a building, your home or otherwise, and you need help, throw something through a glass window or door that is visible from the outside. For example, if someone is attacking you in your home and you can't get out or to a phone, pick up something heavy and pitch it through your front window. The noise will attract the neighbors, particularly if you scream along with it, and they will investigate or call the police. The broken window will pinpoint the source of the problem. (In an emergency, this can be done under less-active circum-stances, as when someone has fallen and been injured or is sick and can't get to a phone for help.) The more noise you make, the greater the chance that someone will hear you and locate the source of the disturbance. Remember when screaming: A simple unadorned scream is not nearly as effective as the word *help.* Screaming may not be enough, particularly in the daytime, where youngsters are screaming in play constantly, and unless someone has a trained ear, he won't be able to distinguish that it is for real. The most effective combination is "Help! Police!" That tells the listener you are in trouble and also suggests a plan of action to him; namely, call the police!

Driving toward help

If you are in a car and can drive, there are many ways of getting help. The circumstances may be many: You're being followed or chased, you're being kidnapped in your own car and have been ordered to drive somewhere, or you're driving and there is someone in the car who you feel is merely waiting for the right place to attack you. Whatever it is, if you keep your head, you can usually get help. Where is that? The obvious source of help is a policeman, but they're spread pretty thin, and there may not be one in your immediate vicinity. Okay—you go to him. Where? To his office, that's where! Keep your horn blaring and pull the flasher button on the dashboard so that your car is blinking like a demented traffic signal; the twin assault on eye and ear will attract attention, maybe that of passing police in their patrol car. Drive to the nearest police, highway-patrol, sheriff's, or ranger station, whichever is closest. On the freeways there are signs that say "Highway Patrol—Next Right," or similar words, depending on which state you're in. In your own area, you should learn where the law-enforcement stations are. You may need the knowledge some day.

If this is a kidnapping, your abductor obviously doesn't know you're heading for the police station (or he would have stopped you), so don't make your play until the last possible moment. Your best bet is to drive right onto the police grounds or into the garage, or whatever is handiest. In an emergency, hit the building or steps with your car. That'll bring 'em out! Use your imagination! In a life-or-death situation, we can't play by the regular rules! Remember, as you arrive there, he is liable to take over the car and zoom off, so as you arrive, grab the keys out of the ignition and throw them away. He'll have to take off on foot right now and isn't going to wait around to clobber you.

There is a far better chance that he'll be caught on foot, too, and you want him caught so he can't come back later at you or another woman.

If you haven't gotten to the police station but see a patrol car en route, the fastest way to stop it is to cut it off or bump it from the rear. Then grab the keys (if possible) and get out and run to the patrol car. Holler "Help!" so that the officer knows you're not trying to assault him. This method is preferred because if you just scream for help as you pass the police car, the kidnapper will have time to clobber you and maybe escape with you in the car, because it's going to take the officer a moment to figure out what is going on, and he can't get into action until he catches up with your car and stops it. (Of course, such dangerous methods as bumping the police car from the rear or wrecking your car are to be used only in emergencies when other methods wouldn't work or you are in immediate fear for your life or great bodily injury. After all, it's hard for a policeman to help you while he's applying a traction splint to his broken leg.)

If the kidnapper is driving the car and you pass a police-man, grab the wheel and try to wreck or stall the car right in front of the officer. Jam on the brake with your left foot. Stand on it! Even if you don't succeed, the swerving car will attract his attention and he will spot the struggle going on. Lying on the horn so that the kidnapper will have to struggle with you will attract the officer's attention, and he'll go after the car. Don't forget deafening and constant cries of "Help!"

Another good place to drive to is a fire station. Here also are trained men who are used to danger and quick decision. A passing fire truck might be handled like the passing police car, but use your head! A sudden stop in front of a speeding fire truck may not be smart!

If you pass a construction site where there are lots of workmen, drive right up to them. Here again are men who are used to physical activity and some danger and are likely to react quickly. Commercial-truck drivers, cab drivers, servicemen, or the "hard hats," all of whom are used to physical activities, are all good bets. Remember to scream, keep the horn blowing, and put on your "flashers." The more attention you attract, the better the chance of help.

Do you see a city bus or streetcar? Cut if off and block its progress. Somebody's got to get out to investigate. How about a taxi stand? A crowded shopping center? If you find one, drive right up on the sidewalk, even hitting a building. You have to attract people *right now* so that your attacker will leave immediately. An apparent accident (running into the building) will attract people on the run. They are much less eager to get to a physical fight scene. Once they are there, however, they will probably help.

In other words, go where there are lots of people. You will have noticed that I didn't suggest you stop some guy on the street as your best bet. Experience has shown that many will just ignore you and brush on by. We've all read stories in which someone in trouble appealed for help and help was refused, or people just stood there and did nothing while the person was attacked or killed. It does happen. There are many reasons why people don't help. They may be physically afraid or don't want to get involved (they might end up as a court witness, for example). Very often, although they are willing to help, they might not be big or strong enough to do you any good. Also, they are taken by surprise and are uncertain as to what is happening, or they think it is merely a husband-and-wife argument, which is not their business. In any case, they are likely to be too slow to prevent your attacker from dragging you back in the car or clobbering you. However, if that's the best available help, use it! Many people *will* come to your aid; many people *will* call the police.

Running toward help

Now suppose you're on foot and need help. All the above reasoning should be considered and applied where possible. But now you have no chariot and fort to help you, and you must run. However, let's run effectively and efficiently. Your pursuer is probably faster than you are and usually has the advantage of not being in a state of panic. You can't afford to make any mistakes or lose any ground that you don't have to lose. Here are a few basic rules to remember when running for your life.

High heels, platform soles, or other fashionable but phys- ically limiting footwear has to go! But don't stop, carefully take them off, and carry them in your hand just as they show in the movies! If the situation is desperate enough to cause you to take them off, you have no spare time. *Kick* them off as fast as you can and get going. You may need the extra couple of seconds. There is one other advantage of not wearing your shoes: Your pursuer can't hear you. If you are not in his sight, he can't locate either your direction of flight or your exact whereabouts. He doesn't know if you are still running or have stopped and hidden somewhere.

Hiding

Maybe we had better digress for a moment and talk specifically about hiding. If you are out of your assailant's sight but have shoes on and he can hear you running, he can also hear you *stop* running and knows just about where you have taken cover. If you are without shoes, however, he doesn't know whether you are still running or have stopped, so *he* doesn't know whether to stop and search or to keep going. If and when you do hide, *stay hidden!* Don't yield to the impulse to peek out to see where he is. Even if he is not looking in your direction, he may see the movement out of the corner of his eye, and you will shortly be "it" when he tags you. Also, the movements you make to peek may create a noise, however slight, that may attract his attention. Even if he doesn't know exactly where it came from, he now knows you are hidden nearby. So don't move or leave your hiding place until a long time has passed and you are sure that he has gone. Don't forget that a couple of minutes under these circumstances can seem like a half hour. Resolve any doubts in favor of staying longer.

Okay, back to running: Always run toward the nearest lights, never into darkness. He can clobber you at his leisure in darkness, and even if your screams have attracted attention, no one can see what is going on or where you are.

Consider running in the street, where you and he are more visible to pedestrians, motorists, and people looking out their windows. Someone running down the sidewalk isn't too unusual, but someone running in the street will always attract attention.

Next, run *straight*. Remember your high-school geometry: The shortest distance between two points is a straight line. Every time you change direction, your pursuer can cut in at an angle and shorten the distance between you. The only time you should change direction is when he is about to grab you and you dodge.

Don't look back! There is an almost overwhelming desire to look behind you to see how close he is. Don't! Every time you do, you slow down, because you cannot run efficiently while your head and upper body are partially turned around, and he can gain a couple of steps on you. All you are going to see if you do look back is him gaining those couple of steps, and you have not accomplished anything.

If you have time to use it, a fire-alarm box means instant action; a police car will also respond. If your pursuer sees you pull the fire alarm, he'll usually take off, because he knows that although the fire engines might take a few minutes to get there, a police cruiser might be in the next block and will get the call also.

What about a telephone booth? Unfortunately, most phones require a coin before the operator can be reached. But if you can get to a phone, use any coin (we've had cases in which the victim didn't have a dime and didn't think of using a quarter!) and dial "operator," *not* the police. It's faster, and she will hold the line open. Tell her "police emergency" and where you are. In case you don't know, the location will be listed on the phone. *Don't hang up!* If the assailant does get to you and drags you off, just drop the phone. The open line can be traced and the operator will send the police. Even if the phone call gets all fouled up, your pursuer won't know it and must take off. A telephone booth is also a temporary fort. If you are being chased and he is going to catch up to you and there is nowhere else to go, at least you can hold him off for a while. The doors are rather easily held from the inside, and you will gain more time for help to get to you. Your screams and the noise he makes trying to break in should attract attention. Another phone to think of is the taxi-stand phone. The dispatcher will get help to you, and a coin isn't necessary.

Using a parked car

If all else fails, and you can't get to help or safety in time, try to get into a parked car. Sometimes the open ones are easily spotted because the door-lock button is in the "up" position or the window is open. If you don't spot these signs, just try each driver's door as you pass the car until you find one that is open and jump in. Lock the doors immediately and your pursuer will be confronted with your new little fort and he can't get to you. Of course, the heavy use of the horn of your borrowed vehicle will add to his peace of mind, and he'll have to get out of there. The horn should bring the owner of the car or some curious neighbors out to look.

BEING CARRIED AWAY

If your assailant is carrying or dragging you off somewhere, the first rule is to make it as difficult as possible for him. He has an unseen enemy—time. The longer he takes, the more chance he has of being discovered, and the better chance you have of escaping or being rescued. One factor you must consider is that even if someone becomes aware of your predicament and comes to your aid, there may be a delay of a couple of minutes between the time your rescuer hears or sees you, realizes what is happening, decides to come to your aid, and gets there. Few people will make an instantaneous decision to run to your aid; usually they hesitate, partially because they can't really believe it is happening, and partially because it takes a little time for the average person to work up his courage to run into physical danger. Like you, they have read of the good Samaritans who have been killed helping a damsel in distress. If he or she calls the police, it's going to take even longer. There is a nightmare quality about an attack in the midst of a busy city: Lights go on and people stare at you from the windows of passing cars, or even from a few feet away, but you are alone and no one is helping you. There may be help on the way, but you have to depend on yourself right now or it will be too late. Here is when you must use your self-defense techniques, and one defense is to delay your assailant's hauling you off to his lair.

Go limp

His usual method is to grab you by the arm and waist or around the throat from the back and force you to walk, however stumblingly and reluctantly, to his car, the traditional bushes, or wherever. Did I say "walk"? How ridiculous! Why help him by walking?! *Go limp right now*. Fake a faint. It will accomplish what you want. It will delay his progress. It isn't nearly as easy to drag a limp figure along the ground as it is to move an upright body walking on its two legs. He almost *has* to drag you; picking someone up from the ground when he or she doesn't want to be picked up is a chore that even firemen, trained in such techniques, find difficult. The heavier you are, the tougher it is. (This will give some of you a brand-new excuse for breaking your diet.) Also—and here we get tricky—he is very much off balance and exposed when he bends over to get a better hold on you, and you can surprise him with a combination of the techniques you will learn later on in this book.

Delay his progress

If he continues to drag you along, again make it as difficult as possible. Grab on to something, like a bush, pole, car bumper, or anything else handy. A sudden stop may even knock him off his feet and cause him to lose his hold. (Then of course, you take off like a scared rabbit and regain as much of your lost ground as you can.) It may be that the handy thing you grab onto may be a rock, heavy stick, garden tool, or something else that can be used as a weapon. Use it then, or hang on to it until a better opportunity comes to use it. A handful of sand or dirt thrown into his eyes is very effective. Another effective way to break loose is to struggle as hard as you can, and then, if that doesn't work, go limp as if you had given up. Then *suddenly* (surprise!) jerk and twist like a maniac. There must be complete surprise, and if there is, you stand a good chance of breaking or loosening his hold.

Escaping the cradle carry

If he is actually carrying you, unless you are very small and light, you can give him fits. If he has you cradled in his arms the way that King Kong hauled off Fay Wray (Figure 7–1), you can make it very difficult by suddenly straightening out your body like an ironing board (Figure 7–2). This prevents him from hauling you in close, which he needs to do to keep his

FIGURE 7–1.

FIGURE 7–2.

93

own balance. If this is done suddenly, he may drop you right there. If not, then by sudden and violent twists and squirms, straightenings and foldings, coupled with attempts to throw yourself over backwards, you can keep him from making much progress or even staying on his feet. While all this is going on, especially if you both fall down, keep very alert for the exposure of his vulnerable areas, especially the groin.

Escaping the "fireman's carry"

He may be carrying you in the fireman's carry, draped over his shoulder with his arm around the inside of your knees (Figure 7–3). This is a very effective carry if the carryee (?) is limp. On the other hand, it isn't too difficult to overbalance the carrier. Straighten up as if you were standing and throw your body backward, forward, sideways, or a well-assorted combination of all of them (Figure 7–4), and he is going to be staggering around like a drunken sailor and will probably have to drop you, if you haven't already pitched yourself off his

FIGURE 7–3.

FIGURE 7–4.

shoulder. (In case you are afraid to drop that far, it's far better than what's awaiting you at the end of his little stroll.) Another good trick is to shove hard with your hands or feet against a passing telephone pole, car, doorway, building, or any solid surface. This will stagger him off balance and possibly cause him to stumble and fall. And while he is off his feet, he isn't taking you anywhere.

Counterattacks

While in the fireman's-carry position, beating on his back with your less-than-hamlike fists is probably not going to cause any reaction more effective than a yawn. Think! What might

95

you use? (Time out: When I say "Now!" put the book down and try to visualize what personal weapons might be effective and against what areas from the fireman's-carry position. Don't cheat; start your training. *Now!*)

You probably came up with several. How about a vicious bite—holding on—on the sensitive muscles covering the back of his ribs? Good! How about fingernails dug deeply into the flesh in the same area or around his waist, particularly if you can get under his clothing and hit the skin? How about a twisting pinch in the same areas? And here's one that probably few of you thought of: reaching back and grabbing for his eyes, or grabbing the corner of his mouth with your fingers and pulling. What a way to turn a man's head! If he is carrying you low, you might get a well-shod toe or your shin into his unprotected groin, and he'll go much lower. Some of you imaginative readers probably thought of others. That's exactly what I want. The more you visualize these situations and possible answers, the more likely you will successfully cope with them in real life.

To sum up, your main concern in being carried is to delay or stop the process while looking for openings to use your other defensive techniques. Of course, it goes without saying that you are also screaming and carrying on while all the poor fellow is looking for is peace and quiet!

WALKING
ON THE STREET
AT NIGHT

Let's devote a few lines to safety factors to be considered if you must walk on the street at night. Whether the purpose is to go to or from a bus stop, your car, or the mailbox, walk the dog, or just take a stroll, it is dangerous. As usual, the first step is preventive. Try to do any necessary walking in the daylight hours. If you do have to walk the dog, do it for his necessities only, not for exercise, and keep close to the house. The dog can be trained to do his thing at a regular spot, but if you allow him to take a leisurely stroll to check up on who's been around the neighborhood lately, he will take all night and visit every tree, hydrant, and pole from there to the county line. Of course, if your dog has the size and disposition of a grizzly bear, much of the danger is cut down. The rapist may become Fido's dinner. A large dog is a comfort at a time like this, but don't count on Fou-Fou the Pomeranian as being much protection. He may be the bravest and fightingest dog in the city, but his size *is* rather against him.

Walk among people . . .

But if you do have to walk on the street at night, try to have someone with you. Even another woman will cut down the danger, as it is the lone woman who is usually the target. But, in any case, plan the safest route; that is, past people and through lighted areas, even if that route is slightly longer. Know the restaurants, shops, gas stations, and other business places that will be open and available for sanctuary or help, as well as the location of telephone booths or police call boxes. Walk close to other groups of people walking if they look safe. (But walking close to a single male or group of males might not be a good idea.) Don't take shortcuts down alleys, across parks, between buildings, through parking lots, or closed service stations. Every chance you don't take moves the odds in your favor. If you are not where a potential attacker is, he can't attack you.

. . . near the curb . . .

Walk near the curb, not close to the buildings. This gives you a better chance to see danger lurking in doorways and alleys. He can't jump you so fast and it's going to take him longer to drag you into shrubbery, doorway, or alley, thus leaving you visible and able to scream for a longer period of time. It also gives you a chance to run into the street so that you can be seen by passing traffic - and he'll be seen too if he tries to attack you or drag you back. If you see possible danger in a parked car, simply cross the street or turn back *before* you get to it. But a word of caution: Don't walk too close to the curb or you could become a target for a purse-snatcher in a car or on a motorcycle who cuts in to the curb and grabs your bag. Stay at arm's length away.

. . . on the left

Try to walk on the left side of the street, that is, against traffic. In this way, an attacker can't follow you in a car and suddenly swerve to the curb alongside you, picking the time and spot to suit himself. By walking against traffic, you deny him these advantages. In any case, when you have to run, head in the opposite direction from which his car is facing, thus forcing him into making a U-turn before he can follow, giving you more time. After he makes his U-turn, consider reversing your direction again. You can reverse faster than he can. If available, turn into a one-way street, the wrong way for him. This will cause him to grind his teeth!

If he is looking for a target of opportunity but doesn't know you are there, you will not be a target. At night, he can't miss the "tap-tap" of female heels on the street, and everyone within a couple of blocks knows that a female target approacheth! Consider removing your shoes or wearing non-tap-tap footwear.

React to early warnings

Possibly one of the most dangerous and stupid games in the world is Russian roulette, in which you put one cartridge in a six-shot revolver, spin the cylinder so that you don't know where it is, put the muzzle to your temple, and pull the trigger. Then the other player does it. You have a 5-to-1 chance of winning, but the result of losing is death. Insane, isn't it? Yet it *is* played occasionally. Women play a game that can be just as dangerous. So many times, after a woman has been attacked, she will say, "I noticed he was following me for several blocks. ..." The point is, *she continued on her way until he caught her!* Now that you think about it, it's incredible, isn't it? The danger is that you never really believe it can happen to you. It's just like Russian roulette! If you think there is danger, *do something* about it. Sure, you may be wrong, but would you rather be raped than embarrassed? If you know, or even think, that someone is following you, get off the street. Go into a store and call some friendly male to pick you up, in the store. Call a taxi. Call the police. If a store or phone booth isn't available, go up to the nearest house with lighted windows. If your follower sees you going into a house he'll probably drop off, as his quarry has dived into its hole. Ring the bell of the house, simply tell them why you rang, and ask them to call your friend, a taxi, or the police. The point is, don't just keep worrying and walking until he catches you!

If you are walking and someone in a car pulls up to ask directions, don't walk up to the car. Stay several feet back so that the person can't snatch your purse and roar off or grab you and jerk you into the car. You can answer questions just fine from the middle of the sidewalk. Don't hang around for a little social chitchat after the necessary directions have been furnished or you will leave yourself available for a longer period of time and could convey the wrong idea. If the guy or guys in the car are rowdy or are making pointed remarks or give you any other signs that they might become a problem, take the same preventive actions we've talked about before: Reverse your direction to leave them headed the wrong way while you head toward people or into a store.

Apply the same general rules if you see someone in a car who appears to have an interest in you make a U-turn back toward you or go around the block and take a second look at you. Act *now*. Assume it to be a danger and take preventive action as described above.

An idea mentioned earlier was to throw something through the window of your house to attract help if someone had you trapped inside. This same principle can be used on the street, but in reverse. In a real emergency, throw something from the street through a lighted window to attract the attention of those inside. They will come out or call the police. If no lighted window is around, toss it anyway. The crash of glass is a great attention-getter. Besides, if you do something like this, your would-be assailant will probably go into shock because he suddenly realizes he has either a very resourceful woman—or a certifiable nut—on his hands, neither of whom he really wants!

Waiting for public transportation

If you have to wait for a bus at night, a lone woman standing under a street light at a bus stop is a highly visible target. It might be better to fade into the shadows or stand close to a pole so that your silhouette does not stand out so obviously. A good safety precaution is to know the bus schedule so that you don't leave the safety of your home, office, friend's house, or movie theater until it's about time for the bus to arrive. This cuts down on your availability. Phone for the bus schedule before you leave your safe place. Of course, if one is available, have some male stand with you until the bus comes.

The same general rules apply to the subway. Stand near the change booth and be visible to the attendant therein. Don't wander down the platform where it is dark or you can't be seen from the booth. If there are other people waiting, move close to them. Don't allow yourself to be isolated. If a situation looks touchy, use a bluff. Step into a telephone booth and pretend to be talking to someone. Wait there for the subway train. Normally, no one will drag you away from the phone, and besides, the booth is also like a little fort.

One way to avoid being alone at night while waiting for the bus or subway, or in the parking lot while going to your car, is to leave the theater, concert, lecture class, or whatever at the same time as the majority of people do, even if it is a little earlier or later than you would have preferred. This gives you quite a bit of company on the way to the parking lot or bus stop.

Aboard public transportation

When you do board the bus or train, sit near the driver, motorman, or conductor. If there are several cars to the train, pick the cars in which there are the most people. Try to sit ahead of the other people in the vehicle so that you are visible to them and they can see anyone making an approach to you. Always sit on an aisle seat for the same reasons of visibility and so you can't be trapped. A man is much less likely to make an approach when there are people watching. He might not feel this constraint, however, if you are sitting to the rear of the people and he could operate in semi-privacy.

Don't be too embarrassed to change your seat, or even change cars, if a situation appears to be developing. Don't suffer in silence if someone is bothering you. If he won't stop when you tell him to, tell him again, only this time in a clear and loud voice. This will attract the attention of others and usually end your problem. This is another case in which he does not care to bask in the limelight.

Stay alert!

The last word about walking on the street, day or night, and a good general rule for all occasions: *Stay alert*. Be aware of what is going on around you so that you can spot an actual or potential danger ahead of time and so that you can take some of the preventive actions we've discussed. If you wait for the danger to hit you, it may be too late.

CHAPTER NINE

SPECIFIC SITUATIONS

The purpose of this chapter is to look at some of the specific situations that experience has taught us are common problems for women, analyzing the factors that often cause the problems, applying the preventive and physical techniques we have learned previously, and adding a few new ones. By becoming familiar with these situations and discussing the answers and alternative answers in advance, you will become far better equipped to handle them if they do come along and far less likely to panic. One of the themes of this book has been to look at a problem, decide how best to handle it, then practice that method ahead of time, thus setting up conditioned reflexes that will come into play in a panic-prone situation, during which your conscious mind isn't functioning too clearly. Let's look at some of the situations.

THE AMOROUS REPAIRMAN

I'm using this term as the generic name for any man who is in your home to repair, install, fix, check, or remove equipment; paint, carpet, build, lay rugs, plumb, or hang paper; in short, any workman in your home. I picked this as one topic because my research for this book indicated that there are often amorous advances, and sometimes attacks, made by persons in this category. Further research into specific incidents, including interviewing some of the repairmen themselves, showed rather conclusively that here was one area in which women often unwittingly contributed substantially to the problem. Prevention is definitely the key to most of these unpleasant situations. Let's 107 discuss the ground rules for women and repairmen.

One of the easiest preventive actions you can take is when a repairman shows up uninvited. Although this unannounced visit is usually legitimate, as is the case with telephone-, gas-, and electric-company workmen checking out trouble or replacing equipment, as well as city and county inspectors of various kinds, you should always make him produce credentials. The fact that he is in a neat uniform is not enough, as uniforms are rather standard and anyone can purchase one that looks almost exactly like any legitimate uniform being used. Be particularly suspicious if the uniform does not have the insignia of the company he claims to represent. If you're at all suspicious, call his company *before* you let him in. This will weed out the phonies, and be sure to call the police if you uncover a phony. However, most of the unpleasant situations resulting from advances made to women come from repairmen actually representing themselves correctly. By and large, repairmen working for major concerns haven't given as much trouble as the repairman working for smaller concerns.

Provocative clothing

If you are not fully and modestly dressed when he gets there, have him wait outside until you are. Provocative clothing has been one of the most common factors that triggers these events. Negligees, short shorts, swim suits, or partial dress may be taken as a signal by the man that you wouldn't be insulted by a pass.

Leave him alone to work.

A complete lack of personal interest in him or his job leaves little opportunity for passes. The majority of problems in this field were started by conversations between the woman and the repairman. To converse with him, the woman has to be standing in his immediate vicinity. Without your immediate presence, a pass is impossible. When a woman hangs around, conversing, holding the flashlight for him, and/or accompanying him to the basement or attic, the repairman may justifiably assume that the woman is giving him a come-on, and if he is inclined that way, he will make a pass. Why do I use the word justifiably? Because if a woman wants him to make a pass (and some women *do* invite passes), that is one way she tells him. Experience has taught him that. So both the woman and the repairman are startled: she when he makes a pass she didn't know she invited, and he when what he thought was asked for is indignantly rejected. Avoid any misunderstanding in this area. Be friendly and courteous, certainly, but in the way it is done in the business world, not socially. Keep your conversation limited to the business at hand, and after all necessary instructions and negotiations are ended, leave him alone. Besides, he will work more efficiently if there are no distractions.

No extras

Here is where your natural friendliness and generosity can get you in trouble. Offering him a coffee break, lunch, or a chance to take a break and talk with you socially all allow openings for the situation you don't want. It seems a shame that we can't do this, for the world certainly needs more friendliness, but for the lone woman, it is dangerous. The man is being paid to work and doesn't expect his visit to be a social one. If you want to furnish a cup of coffee, by all means do so, but do it with a friendly smile and back off again.

Danger signals

If the repairman leaves his area of work to come to you without good reason, the freeze should set in immediately. Get him back to his area right now. This sometimes happens during his coffee break, during which he may come over or even follow you around. He may be naturally friendly, or he may be looking for an opportunity. You don't take a chance.

Personally oriented conversation is another red flag of danger. One of the standard opening moves made by the repairman (and anyone else, man or woman, for that matter) on the make is to turn the conversation by imperceptible degrees into intimate or suggestive channels. Turn it off right then and there and get away from the area so that conversation stops.

If he asks casual questions as to whether anyone else is home or expected, be wary! It is none of his business, and the last thing you ever want anyone to know is that you are alone and unprotected. It would be ridiculous to pretend there is someone else home in a little apartment, where a quick glance around would make a liar out of you, but an indication that you are momentarily expecting a husband, father, brother, boyfriend, or even a girlfriend, will stop any serious advances.

If he does get persistent, a threat to notify his company will often stop him; he would probably lose his job if found out. If he makes a physical pass and is persistent, a threat to make a criminal complaint against him will usually stop all but the worst of them. In any case, if things start to get out of hand, order him out. If he won't get out, you get out and return with help, preferably a large police officer. *Don't stay around:* Once the repairman refuses to get out, he's signalled that he is willing to take risks and could be physically dangerous. If you are going to go out for help, don't *tell* him you are, because *he* might then decide to go for broke, particularly if he panics. Simply wait for your opportunity—if you can—and slip out. If you can't wait, just take off.

PURSE SNATCHERS

Purse-snatching is one of our more common crimes and is at best an expensive nuisance. At worst it can result in your death. Purse-snatchers come in both sexes, all ages, sizes, and shapes. They operate singly, in pairs, and in gangs; on foot, bicycles, motorcycles, and cars. They simply do what the name implies; they snatch your purse and run, or they may knock you down, beat you, mug you, and then grab your purse. Often the purse-snatch is just an excuse for the rough stuff. It can happen in a dark alley or a crowded shopping mall, day or night. In other words, it is an around-the-clock, done anywhere, done by anybody crime. How do you defend against it? You really can't, but we can take certain precautions that will cut down the possibility of its happening and reduce the pain and cost if it does.

First consider your purse, the target in this case. If it is snatched, what does the snatcher get? A couple of bucks, your lipstick, a comb, and a few other items worthless to him. Or does he hit the jackpot? Women tend to carry so much in their purses that a snatcher risks getting a hernia when he grabs it. As part of my research, I checked many purses, and some of them you wouldn't believe! I found some women carry everything they might need for the next three weeks, including all their household and shopping money (on one occasion amounting to over a thousand dollars), all their credit cards, checkbook, uncashed checks, jewelry, and every key they own (as well as a complete filing case of old receipts, bonus coupons, theater stubs, recipes, and so on, most of which the purse-snatcher is welcome to). *Rule: Carry only that which you need for this trip.* Remove all the items you don't intend to use, like gasoline credit cards when you're traveling by bus or with someone else, any extra money, rings, and jewelry you are not going to use; in fact, *don't carry anything valuable that is not needed for that trip.* Then, if the purse is snatched (or merely lost), you lose only the minimum possible. It makes good sense, although I have a sneaking suspicion I'm trying to order the ocean to back up two miles. Consider carrying your money in your bra or in a little flat purse fastened to your waistband.

If your purse is snatched, you have many things to do immediately. Let's say it contained money, house and car keys, check book, uncashed pay or personal checks, and some credit cards. Remember, the house and car keys can be used to enter your house and to steal your car, your checks can be forged and cashed, your uncashed checks endorsed and cashed, and your credit cards used to run up astronomical bills. You can block the use of everything but the money.

Step one. Make a careful inventory of everything contained in the purse, in detail. You should already have a list of all credit-card numbers at home.

Step two. Notify the police of the crime and the property taken. A tremendous number of purse-snatches are never reported, because of the idea that there's nothing the police can do about it. Wrong. By reporting in detail, you alert them to what to look for in pawn shops or in the possession of suspects. By knowing the time, date, and area of the crime, they can add it to the chart showing the activities of the purse-snatchers that they compile from your and other reports. This tells them when and where to concentrate their patrols. If everyone reported these and other crimes (like rape), the police would have far greater success in stopping the criminals. Just think: If every prior victim of your purse-snatcher had reported the crime, maybe he would have been caught before you became a victim!

Step three. Notify your bank of the stolen checkbook and notify everybody whose uncashed check you were carrying so that payment on those checks can be stopped. And, incidentally, be sure you get a replacement, which you might not get if the original is cashed. Immediately notify the credit-card companies of the loss.

Step four. If there was anything in your purse to identify you or where you live, your house keys could be the perfect entry tool for a burglar. Some smart burglars go immediately from the purse-snatch to the home and burglarize it before the victim even makes it back. The thief can also trick you out of your home later. You may get a telephone call from the store in which the theft took place, or from the police, telling you to come to the station and claim your purse. The caller will accurately describe the purse and contents and set a definite appointment for you to come and claim your property, usually right away. You happily report to the appointed spot and find that no one there ever heard of you. After spending some time trying to locate the store official or police detective who called you, you return home, frustrated and unhappy, to find that your home has been thoroughly burglarized. Why thoroughly? Because your caller was the thief, and he had complete assurance that you would be gone for some time. Consider having your locks changed immediately after the theft, but at the very least, keep close watch for the next few weeks. If your address is ascertainable from your purse contents, the thief can easily locate your car in front of your house or in the garage and steal it with the car keys. Consider having your car locks changed.

(By the way, if you carry a miniature license plate that shows your license number as your car-key ring, *get rid of it*. If it's lost or stolen, it tells the thief exactly what car he has the keys for.)

Step five. Take any other action indicated. Use your own imagination and judgment; you know what was in your purse, and the above is only a partial list covering the more common items.

So much for the purse itself. Next, how do you carry it? The worst way is to have it hanging loosely by the strap; this way, it makes a large target, easily scooped up (and, incidently, easily accessible to a pickpocket). Carry it under your arm (with the catch toward your body, making it tough for the pickpocket as well) and hold onto it with your hand. The less visible it is, the less likely it is to attract the attention of the thief. As an aside here, let me mention that the thief is looking for targets of opportunity, and he hangs around stores a lot. When you open your purse to pay for an item, be secretive about it. Don't show your money or other valuables. Handle the transaction as if you were a poker player looking at your hand.

Because of the many ways this crime can be committed, I can't give you any sure-fire way of preventing it. Sometimes, if you are alert, you can see it being set up. If you notice someone, usually a young male, watching you, walking parallel to you across the street, or following you, there is a chance that you are the target. Your best bet is to get with people (as in a store or bus stop), get on a bus, hail a taxi, or do anything else that comes to mind to break his opportunity. Don't immediately start running; that could trigger him to act immediately. Try to make your move when you are nearer help. If you are with people, take a firmer grip on your purse. (If you are alone, it is probably smarter to let him get it on the first grab rather than have him fight you for it.)

This brings us to the next point: Do you or don't you fight for control of the purse? It depends upon how big and strong you are, who is grabbing it, and whether there are people around. You be the judge. But should you risk serious injury (many of them play *rough!*) for a $15.95 purse, $3.45 in cash, and a load of junk you could replace for $5.00? Besides, usually the purse is thrown away and you have a fair chance of recovering everything but the money. If you are alone on the street, fighting is probably a poor idea, because the purse-snatcher has time to clobber you and take the purse anyway without anyone interfering. If you are in a crowd, however, he has to grab and run, or someone is liable to grab him. Again, use your own judgment.

If he grabs it and gets away, one of the errors made is that the victim usually takes a couple of steps along his line of flight, then stops to tell someone about it, losing sight of the thief. Train yourself right now to follow him as far as you safely can (but don't catch up and get clobbered), shouting for someone to stop him. You might get lucky. There are still a lot of people who will get involved. Get a description of him. Tell yourself—*out loud*—what he is wearing. (By saying it out loud, you have a far better chance of remembering it correctly later.) Note the last place you have him in sight. If he gets into a car, try to get the license number; even one letter or number will help, and write it down as fast as possible so you won't get mixed up. If you lack paper and pen, draw it in the dirt, or in the dust on a parked car or a building, or write it on your hand. Then call the police. The faster you call them, the better chance a patrol car has of spotting the thief on the street. The helicopter patrol has had great success with this.

OBSCENE TELEPHONE CALLS

This section covers not only obscene and suggestive telephone calls, but also those that consist merely of heavy breathing or just plain silence, all of which can turn into the obscene call. This subject kept cropping up in my research for this book, as the calls are always an unpleasant nuisance and are often frightening. Any attempt to throw a step-over toehold on a guy on the other end of a telephone is destined to fail, so we have to approach the situation from the standpoint of prevention, psychology, identification, and possible prosecution.

We start, as always, with prevention. In your telephone listing, as on your mailbox, don't advertise that you are a woman. "Mary E. Bratwurst" will attract the attention of one of these callers, but "M. E. Bratwurst" will be identifiable to your friends but not of any help to the weirdo. In some areas you can have your name and telephone number listed without the address. This will keep your location a secret, so that even if he reaches you by phone, he can't get to you physically. In some areas you can get an unpublished number, which can be obtained from Information but will not be listed in the telephone directory. Or you can get an unlisted number, which can't be obtained at all.

One of the most important precautions is to avoid *ever* giving out personal information over the phone unless you know exactly whom you are talking to. If the caller claims a wrong number and asks what your number is, merely ask what number he is calling. Whether he answers with your number or a different one, say, "I'm sorry. You have the wrong number" in a polite voice and hang up. Don't give him your number to show him that he has the wrong one. If he asks for someone who does not live there, tell him so, and if he then asks, "Who is this?" your response is not your name but "Who are you looking for?" If the name is unknown to you, say there is no one there by that name and politely hang up. Above all, don't let him know you are alone. If the call is for someone else in the house who is not there, be noncommittal and say that he or she is not available right now and that you will have the party call back. Take the caller's number, and that should end it, legitimate or not. Be sure your own children and the baby sitter have the same instructions. The sitter should never tell anyone that he or she is alone with the children.

So much for prevention. Now for the psychology. In most cases you will get one or a few calls, usually by someone you don't know and who doesn't know you. Many youngsters pick a number out of the directory or simply dial at random and hassle anyone who answers. Usually, all you can do is discourage the caller by taking any fun or satisfaction out of his little game. The cardinal rule is to stifle your natural curiosity (not easy!) and as soon as it is established that the call is in either the obscene or nuisance category, *hang up!* Don't talk at all; *hang up!* This normally will discourage the caller (who may be female, by the way) because there is no fun in it. He wants you to get mad, get upset, or Oh Joy! maybe he has found someone who will listen to his sick droolings! If you do listen, you will probably be a target for some time to come, because he isn't going to lose a jewel like you! Maybe you'll do it again! All he really wants is an audience. Don't try to discourage him by calling him all sorts of names or telling him off; that is talking to him, and he gets his kicks out of hearing your rage. One gag going around is that you should say, "Just a minute; wait 'til I get a cigarette," on the theory that that will throw him. Don't. You are still encouraging him and he may become a permanent part of your daily routine. If the calls continue, you might let him talk for a moment and then say, "This is the one, Operator" in a loud voice, or whisper, apparently to someone nearby, "Turn on the recorder, John." He'll probably disappear from your life, because being identified is not on his agenda. Another gimmick you can try: Just before you hang up, turn your head away from the mouthpiece as if you were talking to someone else in the room and casually remark, "Oh, it's just the weirdo again." Then hang up. This hurts his ego and also tells him something his mind won't accept, because he *is* a weirdo. He may go on to greener pastures.

One of the most useless techniques often taught is to suddenly blow a police whistle into the mouthpiece, which is supposed to send him up the wall. Forget it. The whistle may send your cat to the top of the drapery rod, but your caller will merely wonder what the background noise is. It doesn't work. Your phone is designed to cut out loud, high-pitched sounds.

If the calls don't stop, report them to the business office of your telephone company and change your telephone number, requesting that when the recording "You have reached a discontinued number" comes on the line, it not be followed by "that number is changed to ..." If your caller does have your name, he can get the new number from Information, but this *will* stop the caller who merely picked your number accidentally. If you do "unlist" your number and the calls continue, you know it is someone you know and have given your new number to.

If your unknown caller knows you and is deliberately setting out to keep you awake or otherwise harass or annoy you, it may not be enough to take the fun out, because he (or she) may have a different intent from the one that the run-of-the-mill caller has. He is out to bother you, be it for revenge, punishment, or some other reason. In these cases, as well as the one concerning the persistent caller you can't get rid of, the answer lies with the telephone company and/or the police. So now we move into the field of identifying the caller so he can be stopped. I mention the police in case the caller has made actual or implied threats, or for some other reason you feel that you are in danger. In these cases, cut the police in from the beginning.

To get the machinery going (and we'll talk about the telephone company only, as the police will take it over if they are involved), you must notify the business office of the telephone company of your problem and they will advise you from there. But give them as much as possible to work on. If it is evident that the caller is out to deliberately harass and annoy you, you probably have a pretty good idea as to which one of your friends is mad at you (or, if you are rather active, how many). By limiting the field, the authorities have a far better chance of identifying your eager communicant and paying him a cordial visit. In any case, if you begin to get these calls, have a pencil and paper near the phone, and as soon as one comes in, hang up and immediately log it in as to date, time, and any other information, such as the *exact* words used (don't get embarrassed and fail to write out the exact language), whether it was a man's or woman's voice, the approximate age, any background noise, and so on. This will start to form a pattern that will be of great help in both the identification and possible prosecution of your caller, if it goes that far. There are things that a trained investigator can deduce from your log that you might not think of. He observes the pattern and may discover that the calls always come in just after your husband or boyfriend leaves, just as you arrive home, or immediately after you turn out your lights. This last one may indicate that someone is watching you. The calls may all come in at the same approximate time or only on certain days, indicating the availability pattern of the caller. This really helps those who are trying to help you. If you look your log over carefully, you might get a better idea than the investigator.

The ability to trace calls, which is now called "line identification," varies from locality to locality, depending on what kind of equipment the telephone company has in your particular exchange area. (The exchange is the first three numbers of your telephone number [after the area code].) However, the capacity is increasing constantly, and in more and more areas instantaneous line identification can be made by computer. The computer can print out the number of the calling and called parties and the time and duration of the call, and it can keep a record of it. This will enable the telephone company and the police to identify your talkative friend and give him something other than you to think about.

But, in essence, the best thing to do is *hang up immediately!*

THE THEATER MASHER

This is somewhat similar to the situations we discussed concerning buses and trains. Both involve the woman sitting alone, but this has the added danger of darkness, and darkness gives some of these weirdos courage. Ordinarily the most you will be subjected to in a movie theater is annoyance and personal outrage rather than danger, unless the theater is almost deserted, in which case I wouldn't advise you go in or stay at all, particularly if there are no ushers.

When in the theatre, sit by the aisle so that you can get out easily and so that any struggle or activity is much more likely to be noticed. The main floor is always far safer than the balcony, which usually has the fewest people and is out of sight of the ushers. Avoid dark corners or any area of vacant seats in the balcony or rear of the theater. If you notice any rowdies or loud-talking men, stay well away from their area and sit well behind them so that you won't be spotted.

If someone bothers you, change your seat, always moving behind him. If he persists, call the usher or go out and get him. Use the "loud and clear voice" technique to draw attention to you and your problem, followed by a change in seats. Everyone in the theater will be alerted, and not many mashers will continue under these circumstances and would probably run into some active opposition from the audience if he did. If the approach is really bad, scream and try to stand up so that everyone can spot the scene of the disturbance. (Here's a really great opportunity to use your whistle!) He'll have to leave now, because a scream or whistle will probably bring the usher, manager, or the police, not to mention help from the audience.

Your best bet, of course, is to go in the company of others, in which case the problem probably won't arise, and if it does, two of you can handle it better than one.

THE LAUNDROMAT

The laundromat is a potential danger spot at night, particularly late at night. The night prowlers know it is a source of supply of lone women for them, because they are the ones who use it the most. The best safety precaution is to arrange for someone to accompany you and do his or her clothes at the same time. If not, make sure you are visible. Stay near the front and don't get trapped in a spot out of sight of the street. If someone makes you suspicious of his intentions by his actions or attitudes, move now; don't wait until your suspicions are confirmed. Move to a more visible location, or, if necessary, just leave. You can come back later for your clothes. So many times the police hear that same story, "I saw him watching me but I didn't think he would do anything. . . . I had to wait for my clothes to finish. . . ." You can think of many more standard excuses for not doing anything until too late. Remember the chapter on assertiveness. Prevention! Don't take the chances.

ELEVATORS

Another danger spot is the automatic, or self-service, elevator. This is a common arena for everything from suggestive remarks to molesting to robbery and/or rape. This applies to both the apartment-house elevator and the office-building elevator. The latter is particularly dangerous at night, when few people are around the area.

The attacker merely has to push the "stop" button to halt the elevator between floors and he has reserved a little room from which you can't escape. Your screams may be unheard, or if heard, not locatable; in any case, no help can get to you. The attacker is in no hurry; he can escape onto any floor he chooses while sending you and the elevator to another landing or push you out while he rides to a point of escape.

These may be planned crimes or may be crimes of opportunity. If the assailant sees you alone, the idea might strike him. The key word, as usual, is *alone*. Try to avoid entering an elevator with a lone man. Wait for the next trip, particularly if something about him makes you nervous. Here is another time to play your hunches. Don't get aboard. If you feel embarrassed about not boarding or changing your mind and getting out, snap your fingers as if you just remembered something, shake your head in exasperation, and leave. If your suspicions are strong enough, leave the premises or head for people. If you are aboard the elevator and become suspicious of the other's intentions or attentions, don't wait for your floor; get off as soon as possible, before his ideas jell. If possible, try to get off where there probably will be other people so he can't take any positive action. If a suspicious man enters the elevator from another floor, simply step out on that floor.

If you run into trouble, there is usually an emergency-alarm button that you can push to set off an audible alarm. It probably won't bring instant help, but it may frighten him off. It is obvious from the above that the safest place for you on the elevator is by the buttons. It keeps you nearer the alarm or the button to stop at the next floor to get off if you see a problem developing, and it may keep him from impulsively going into action. Push every button in case you missed the one for the next available floor.

CHAPTER
TEN

COMMERCIAL
PROTECTIVE
WEAPONS

I have noticed many advertisements, particularly in the pulp magazines, attempting to sell women various devices "guaranteed" to repel the unwanted intruder or attacker. Many of the weapons are useless; others might work—if you ever got a chance to use them. Let's talk generally about one of the toughest problems to overcome in this area: how to bring the weapon into play. Let's say you have a gun, knife, ice pick, tear-gas gun, cattle prod, police whistle, blackjack, or whatever. Here comes your eager assailant, suddenly accosting you. What do you do? You dig into your purse or your pocket, haul out your weapon, and vanquish your opponent, who in the advertisement is always shown cowering away from the little woman or running away in terror. In real life, what chance do you think you would have of getting to the weapon? As soon as you dive into the purse, he's going to clobber you or grab the purse, or if you did get to it, your violent motions will have tipped him off as to your intentions, and the chances of your winning the wrestling match for the weapon are rather remote. If you do have a weapon, probably your only chance to use it is if you are carrying it in your hand at the time of the attack, but it will be visible to him. The weapon must be innocent-looking or he will go for it first. In other words, it has to be carried "at the ready" and not noticeable to him. This may be done if you are walking to your house from the bus stop at night, but normally you wouldn't have the weapon in your hand.

The police whistle

One of the effective weapons you might use is a police whistle. The theory is that when you are accosted, you blow the whistle loud and long and he will vacate the area right away.

He may, too, because a police whistle is designed to be loud and carry a long distance and is rarely mistaken for anything else. Some women carry the whistle on a chain around the neck, which is a fine idea, or around the wrist, which is a better idea. This keeps it ready for immediate use, and you won't lose it during the excitement or activity of an emergency. *Caution:* The chain around your neck should be a light one that will break if someone grabs it and pulls. Otherwise, you can be hauled around by the chain as if you were on a leash, or even strangled with it. However, about the only way you're sure to be able to use it is if you carry it in your mouth. So, carry it in your mouth while walking to your home! You may think this is strange and silly advice, but the value of this book is that it is realistic. If you are assaulted suddenly, there is an excellent chance you would never get to your whistle, even if it is around your neck or wrist. So, the *best* place is in your mouth. Now we can get practical: A woman walking around socially with a whistle in her mouth is going to be thought a wee bit strange. (If not, she moves in a fascinating circle of friends.) So modify the *best* solution in the light of practicality. We do know that a whistle buried in your purse is useless. So, when you are walking from the bus stop to your home at night, carry the little rascal in your hand, ready for instant use. If you see a situation developing, such as that of a man coming up to you in a way you don't like, *then* put it into your mouth until the situation clears. If he has innocent intentions, he won't even notice the whistle. If he *is* a bad guy, he will, and he'll probably decide you are: 1) ready, 2) an undercover cop, 3) or nuts, and therefore too unpredictable to attack. You can't lose!

One more thing about a whistle: As when you are screaming, there is always a chance that he will knock you flat to stop that noise, but in an attack, what have you got to lose? Also, don't forget that the whistle can be used effectively when you are in your house, the theater, on a bus, or anyplace where you have to attract attention. Incidentally whistles are very cheap but very effective. Why not have more than one? Keep one in the car, one at home by your bed, and one to carry. Isn't it silly the way we economize sometimes?

Aerosol sprays

There are various aerosol sprays of tear gas or other liquids advertised as the end and answer to the problem. However, mere possession is illegal in many states; in others, including California, you must pass a course and be licensed to carry one. Be careful. Some of them, unlike Mace and tear gas, are injurious to the eyes, and very often in the struggle when you use them you will get a pretty good dose yourself. Some are effective if you can get to use them. An alternative that I think is pretty clever is an aerosol can of red paint. If squirted into his eyes, it will temporarily blind him, and no matter where you hit him, only a colorblind policeman could miss the suspect on the street afterward.

I tried out one of the "electric batons" not too long ago. This is a takeoff on the cattle prod and consists of a tube, like a three-cell flashlight's, containing batteries. When it's turned on and touching somebody, it gives an electrical shock. I was able to hold onto the thing, taking the full charge, with nothing but a little discomfort. It certainly startled me for a moment, but it did not disable or hurt me at all. It is a neat parlor trick but would not stop a determined attacker.

Firearms

Many women have asked me whether they should purchase a gun. I'd have to answer "No." The accurate use of a firearm under stress is difficult to teach police officers, even after long hours of training, yet some women want to carry a firearm around with no training at all. To be effective and accurate with a gun, under stress or not, takes a lot of training and practice, and if the bullet misses your assailant, it's not going to say "Oh, shucks!" and drop to the floor; it's going to keep going, even through the wall, until it hits something, maybe the wall, your color TV—or your husband, kids, or roommate. Think also of some frightening recent statistics that

125

show that a handgun in the home is about six times more likely to kill a family member than the attacker.

And let's say something about firearms training that many self-defense "experts" don't tell you: Long hours of expert instructións at a range, firing at a stationary target from a careful, steady stance, with plenty of time to aim each shot, may make you an expert—an expert at hitting targets that don't move, curse, run at you with a knife, or shoot back. Add stress, if not outright panic, to the situation, and you're lucky if you can even pull the trigger, let alone hit your target. If that doesn't discourage you, add the fact that it will probably be at night, when you can't even see your gunsights to aim. This is reality. (Next time you are on the range, try just blasting away at your target in a real hurry, without using your sights. Okay? Now move up to within five feet of it and try again. Be sure a large area around your target is clear! Don't feel bad; even trained law-enforcement officers have major problems in this area.)

Here is another reason for caution. One woman wrote me, "In Medford, Oregon, my neighbor was beaten by a prowler when she walked in and surprised him in her living room. She had heard him walking around and she came out of her bedroom with her husband's .22-caliber revolver. The sight of the gun angered him and he took it away and beat her with it." This is part of my reluctance to suggest a gun. (Just for practice, constructively criticize the Medford woman's actions and pick out the errors. *Try it! Don't* read ahead—try it first! I'll wait.)

Let's check you. First, she came out of her bedroom, giving him a chance at her. Second, she had a gun and *walked within reach of him.* Third, if she had been planning to use the gun, she should have fired when he failed to stop and moved toward her. You got 'em all, didn't you? They were obvious. *But it happened*—in real life!

I do not recommend guns for several other reasons. There are legal requirements to be met before you can get a permit to carry a gun, and severe penalties for carrying it without a permit. There are also severe legal penalties for the wrongful use of a gun, even against the bad guys in some instances, that you should be aware of. Add to that the need for many hours of expert stress training before you can use it effectively. I think I have made my point. Make your own decision, but don't try to use a gun until you have been trained by an expert and know the legal limitations.

Stabbing weapons

Much the same arguments can be used about carrying a knife. Legally, you might be subject to penalty for carrying a concealed weapon; the effective use of a knife in combat is not easy, and it may be taken away and used against you. The same thing applies to an ice pick.

Women are constantly being told to jab their assailant with a hatpin. In the first place, hatpins aren't easy to find today. In the second place, where and how do you carry it? In the third place, they might be excellent for discouraging a masher type, but a hatpin used to inflict deep injury is usually ineffective. It would probably bend or break, and it is very difficult to hold firmly enough to get the power to pierce flesh deeply, let alone through the clothing. It can, however, be used to dig and scratch. (If you are the showoff type, you might try scratching your initials on your assailant for later identification.)

On the other hand, if you are being attacked and these weapons come to hand, use them if the situation is deadly enough. My objection is to the *carrying* of them as a defensive device, for the reasons stated. In the case of an attack, any weapon can be of value, even if it is not called a weapon. For example, a ballpoint pen, sharpened pencil, rat-tail comb, nail file, or any similar object, like a sharp stick, can be used as a dagger.

The baseball bat

One of the deadliest weapons you can keep in your home is the good old-fashioned baseball bat. No, I'm not being funny!

Even if you're not athletic and strong, few people care to move in close to a poised baseball bat. It has a long reach and is very heavy. Even if your attacker blocked the blow, he would probably wind up with a broken arm or hand. Keep the bat poised and high and most people won't take the chance of coming within range. Tell him your batting average is over .400. If he's a baseball fan, he'll leave.

BASIC
PRINCIPLES

A revolver is useless for defense unless you know how to load, aim, and fire it correctly, and to be able to do this you must first study and practice the correct stance, grip, trigger squeeze, sight picture, and breathing, and then put them all together. The same holds true for the self-defense techniques set forth hereafter in this book. There are certain basic principles that must be practiced, understood, and put together before the self-defense techniques can be successfully used. They are the same principles that underlie the success of any physical activity. Your success in applying the techniques set out hereafter is tied directly to your understanding of these basic principles. *Don't skip this chapter; these techniques won't work if the basic principles are not followed!* To women, this background is of particular importance, because one reason the average woman is physically inferior to the average man is that she hasn't been taught these basic principles. Granted, if you asked the average man to name and explain them, his answer would be "Huh?"; the difference is that he has learned to do most of them instinctively, based on those thousands of hours of practice mentioned earlier. Also, long experience has taught me that even good athletes can better their techniques by a study of the basic principles, by bringing to their conscious minds that which they know only instinctively. So, we will discuss each principle separately, and we will be constantly referring to them in later chapters.

Balance

Our first basic principle is balance. It is probably the most important one: It must be present for all the other principles to work. Watch a baby, newly able to walk, push something. He falls flat on his plump little diaper, because he is off balance, i.e., directly facing his "opponent." Try this: Stand *with your feet together* and have someone push you from the side; you will stagger off balance. Return to position and successively take the push from the other side, the front, and the back, returning to position each time. You will stagger off balance when pushed from any direction of the compass, because you are not in a balanced position to start with.*Try it!*

Now, before we go any further, let's describe a balanced position. (All directions given are for a right-handed person. If you are a southpaw, reverse all directions.) Stand with your feet about shoulders-width apart with the toe of your right foot about even with the heel of your left foot. Your knees should be slightly flexed, your waist slightly bent forward, and your hands raised in front of you. Twist your feet and body a little to the left so that you are looking at your opponent pretty much over your left foot (Figure 11–1).

FIGURE 11–1.

FIGURE 11-2.

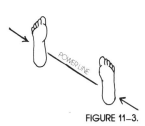

FIGURE 11-3.

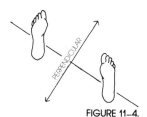

FIGURE 11-4.

Now look at our football player (Figure 11–2). He is in an exaggerated balanced position, because if he were not, he would shortly be a resident of Section 16, Row 5. A diagram of his foot positions shows this (Figure 11–3). It would take not much less than an army tank to move him in the direction of the arrows. In other words, he is on perfect balance to resist a push along a line drawn directly between his feet, which we will hereinafter call the "power line." However, if a line is drawn *perpendicular* to (at right angles to) the power line, he will be vulnerable to a push along that perpendicular line (Figure 11–4). *Try it!* However you place your feet, you will be able to resist a push along the power line but will be a pushover along the perpendicular. There is, therefore, no perfectly balanced position, and we must shift our position to meet the expected direction of the attack. By the same reasoning, if you want to get results, don't bother to push your opponent along his power line; push or pull him along the perpendicular. Those of you who have practiced judo throws have used this principle and probably didn't know it. Want a good example? Watch an untrained girl (or boy) throw a baseball. Awkward and ineffective, isn't it? Now note: The girl is probably directly facing her target, i.e., looking straight down that perpendicular line. Even a trained baseball player would look awkward from this position. *Try it!* Now get into a balanced position and do the same thing. Note the ease of the throw, and note something else that is going to become very important to you: Part of the power in your throw came off your back leg. *Try it!* That's why I call it the "power line." Try taking a push or giving a push along your power line—you'll find that you are pushing off your back foot. That's why our baby fell down on his diaper—no back foot to furnish the anchor for the power. So, all our techniques *must* be used from a balanced position.

Use all your muscles

FIGURE 11–5.

FIGURE 11–6.

So we come to our second principle: *Use all your muscles.* Let's go back to our untrained girl throwing a baseball. We've now taught her Principle 1, Balance, and she does much better, but her throw is still embarrassingly weak and still awkward. Note that only her arm is in motion. Now switch on the TV set and watch a professional baseball pitcher do the same thing. He, like our girl, is in a balanced position, working from his power line, but there the resemblance ends. Just before he throws, he winds up every muscle he owns: He rears back, swings his right arm 'way behind him, raises his left leg and left arm, and twists his upper body around. He's wound himself up like a spring, all cocked and ready to go! (Figure 11–5). Then he "pulls the trigger" and lets fly with every muscle in his body. The body unwinds with explosive force, and the ball travels at upwards of 90 miles per hour toward the plate, propelled by his arm, but backed by the full power of his body. He even throws himself off the mound by the powerful follow through of his right leg! (Figure 11–6).

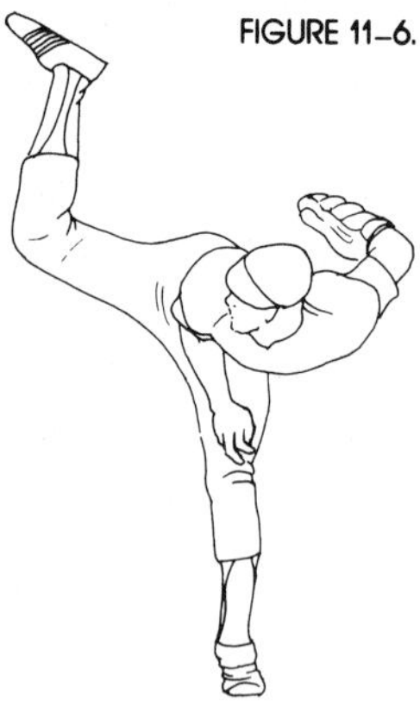

That is Principle 2, *the use of all your muscles*, from, of course, a balanced position. You therefore apply Principles 1 and 2 *every* time you push, pull, hit, or kick, to supply power you never dreamed you possessed. Use *all* your muscles. You have none to spare. Note that the back leg in your power line is the key. Look at Figure 11–7. Our girl is pushing her adversary, but it is obvious that she does not have much power, because she is definitely not using all her available muscles. Note, however, that what power she has is coming from the power-line, off her left leg. Now look at Figure 11–8. It is apparent that she has much more power than before because she is on better balance for the job at hand and is putting every possible muscle into play. Your thigh muscles are the most powerful muscles in your body. Use them. Notice how she is utilizing them. Note also that when she is pushing, the power is transmitted from her back foot, up the leg and torso to the points of contact, in this case her hands and shoulder. Of course, you won't be spending *all* your time crippling and maiming aspiring assailants, so why not use these two principles in your other daily work? Next time you have to shove a piece of furniture around, lift a heavy box, or simply push open a heavy door in a department store, do it from a balanced position and use all your muscles. *Try it!* (I can see it now, the careless reader approaching a department-store door, rearing back, lifting her left leg. . .)

FIGURE 11–7.

FIGURE 11–8.

Attack your opponent's weakest spot

Now we'll look at Principle 3: *Attack your opponent's weakest spot.* It makes no sense for you to pit your strength against him or to meet him on even terms. That would be a tug-of-war between a Volkswagen and an Army truck: The outcome is a foregone conclusion, but that's the way the cards were dealt. So how do we handle it? Picture a man's arms suddenly grabbing you around your waist from behind, his right hand grasping his own left wrist. You place your right hand over his, finger for finger, and try to pry his four fingers loose with your four fingers. Zero. The VW versus the truck. Now apply Principle 3. Look at his hand. What is the weakest point? The little finger, of course! So now we apply Principles 1, 2, and 3 (again note that we bring *all* of them into play *every* time); you grasp his little finger with your *two* hands (*both* of them), then from a balanced position, using *all* your muscles, pry off just his little finger. You will note that if his little finger goes, the rest of the hand will follow. This is a well-known scientific principle. Of course, if he is stubborn and just lets his little finger take the rap, you will hear a sharp "crack!" The little finger will just lie there. Then you grab his *next* finger with both hands and repeat the process. Eventually he will run out of workable fingers and you will be free. We not only attack the weakest point, in this case the little finger, but we also apply *all* our muscles to it. Note that you added extra power by adding your other hand, and don't forget to drive off that rear leg in the power line. It takes a while to get everything working together, but it will come.

Use your opponent's weight and momentum against him

In logical progression, we come to Principle 4: *Use your opponent's weight and momentum against him.* Again, we are simply not going to meet this guy on even terms because the terms are *not* even. He is probably bigger, heavier, and stronger than you. But even professional football players, evenly matched, use this principle. Watch the offensive team protect the passer. When a defensive player breaks through the line and rushes the passer, he is more than his listed 265 pounds. Sure, the protector is listed at 271 pounds himself, but because of his opponent's momentum, he's going to meet a lot more than that; even if he did successfully meet and stop the charge, think of the tremendous punishment he would be taking. So, he applies Principle 4: He does not meet the rush head on but starts moving *with* the rush, giving ground, and deflecting the rush to the outside of the passer, using relatively little force to push the oncoming linesman off his intended line of direction. The force was supplied by the *other* guy, and it was used against him. You see this same principle used several nights a week on the TV late, late show. In every Western there is a big brawl, and sooner or later one of the bad guys rushes murderously at the hero, who gives ground, drops to his back, places his foot on the villain's fat stomach, and propels him spectacularly over his head, usually through a poker table. Principle 4! (If you haven't seen this, you go to bed too early, undoubtedly lead a clean, sensible life, and probably don't need this book.) I don't recommend your trying that one until you've had a lot of practice: The timing must be precise, and besides, there probably wouldn't be a poker table within a mile of you. However, if you are being wrestled to the ground, don't let this guy land on top of your delicate frame, knocking the breath and any remaining ability to fight out of you. Instead, on the way down, grab him, twist around, and drag him around with you, preferably so that *he* lands on the bottom, or at least not on top of you. Your 113 pounds are easily capable of turning his 194 pounds around in mid-air. Why? Because he has no *balance,* and it takes only a few pounds of thrust to turn him in full flight. Another application of Principle 4: If he is running at you (Figure 11–9) or you are being shoved backward violently, instead of opposing his force, grab him just as he makes contact, step back fast, and turn him as you pull him by (Figure 11–10). He should at least be staggered (Figure 11–11). His own momentum supplied the force.

FIGURE 11-9.

FIGURE 11-10.

FIGURE 11-11.

Surprise and speed

And finally, Principle 5, a bonus, really, because there are two for the price of one: the Siamese twins, *surprise* and *speed*. These two are inseparable; neither will work without the other. Let's talk about them separately first. *Surprise* really has to do with reaction time. You've read many times in traffic-safety articles about safe stopping distances; if you remember, one of the factors is the length of time it takes you to react and hit the brake *after* you have seen the danger. Although it varies with individuals, it takes a measurable length of time, averaging three-fourths of a second. This means that if you surprise your opponent with a sudden move, it will take him a good part of a second to react to and block it, giving you that much free time in which to operate, so that your blow will land before he has a chance to get his guard up. What if *your* reaction time is slow? Who cares?! It could be six minutes or two hours, because your reaction time doesn't figure in this part of the game anyway. The time you take making up your mind what to do and getting your brain to tell the necessary muscles to do it all takes place before you begin to move, no matter how long that took. He can't even perceive his danger until your body starts to move. *Then* he starts his reaction. His three-fourths of a second doesn't even start until then, well after your reaction time is already over! For example, you could probably move your hand from your waist to his face in under one-eighth of a second, far less time than it takes him to react to block you. "Aha," you say. "How is it then that whenever I playfully spar with a male he easily catches my hand before I can connect with his face?" Easy. *Surprise* is totally lacking. He is ready, expectant, and with his thousands of hours of experience (remember?) can outrace you to the target. Also, you are probably making one of the most common mistakes known: You are "telegraphing" your moves. This simply means that by a little preliminary movement, such as a shifting of the feet, a darting glance at your target, an almost imperceptible tensing of your muscles, or any one of a thousand physical signs, you are telling your opponent, "I'm making my move now," and he can start to react immediately, thus shortening his reaction time and giving you less time in which to operate. Take these two facts—that he is ready

139

for your attack and that you tell him in advance when you are going to make your move, and possibly even where—and it adds up to "You lose." There is no easy answer to this problem, but I will point out that when it is for real there will be so much movement that your moves will be fairly well masked, and the moves you will be learning here will not be the ones the assailant will expect.

Another factor comes into play here. A man will be expecting resistance from you and will be alert for the obvious (that's why the old reliable standby for women, the "knee to the groin," rarely works; since he was a little kid he has learned to protect against this most-feared of the assaults upon him). So, you must "set up" your surprise. In boxing, this is called "feinting" (which differs from "fainting," which is what you may feel like doing). A feint is merely a move to throw your opponent off guard, an apparent attack at one point while the real objective is another. You have often used feints when you were a little girl and were trying to run around a playmate in a game of tag, pretending to start around her left side, and when she moved in that direction, suddenly darting to the right. This, of course, left her moving in the wrong direction. A good example in our field of self-defense would be if you made a sudden pass at an attacker's eyes with your hand and, as his guard and attention went up to meet this danger, suddenly aimed your knee at his groin. You feinted him out of position. The basic rule is that if he knows what you're trying to do, he can probably block it.

A word of caution: If you try a move and it fails, don't try the same thing again immediately, because now he's ready for it. You might feint him out of position later, but try something else first.

Now for the other half of the twins, *speed*. This simply means you must follow up quickly to retain the advantage of the surprise. Remember that girlhood game of tag? Suppose you feinted your friend to the left and then moved to the right, but instead of darting past her, you hesitated a moment. Your playmate would then have recovered and you would shortly thereafter be "it." You lost the advantage of surprise by failing to follow up with speed. Surprise is only good for a fraction of a second. The follow-up move has to be within that time or the surprise is gone and you are back where you started. *Surprise and speed.* Add them to your other basic principles and you have a good chance of making our techniques work.

A quick review:

1. Balance.
2. Use all your muscles.
3. Attack your opponent's weakest spot.
4. Use your opponent's weight and momentum against him.
5. Surprise and speed.

These then, are the basic principles you must have in mind *every* time you try to work one of the techniques. Don't just flip ahead to the next chapters and ignore them. Think about them. Understand them. Take my word for it: *The techniques probably won't work without these principles' being used.* So refer to them occasionally until you really understand them. A good way to do this is to see how well they apply to almost any routine physical action you take in your daily life, like pushing heavy furniture, opening a stuck jar lid, pushing a heavy box to a top shelf, or pushing your vacuum cleaner. Don't just read this and say "Good idea." Consciously think about them and consciously use them in daily tasks. Not only will you be surprised as to how much easier some of your tasks will be, but you will be training your mind and body to instinctively use these principles for all future needs, household or defense. You can't lose!

CHAPTER TWELVE

VULNERABLE AREAS

This chapter starts getting into the meat of our self-defense techniques and is at the same time part of your necessary background knowledge. A common phrase running through self-defense books is "strike him" or "kick him." They fail to tell you *exactly what* weapon to use (usually assuming your fist or toe) or *exactly where* to hit. A blow can be delivered by many different personal (natural) weapons and can be effectively delivered to many different locations. ("Personal" or "natural" weapons, which I will discuss in the next chapter, are weapons that can be formed by your body members, such as fists, feet, elbows, knees, head, and so on.) This and the next chapter are designed to teach you to recognize the many personal weapons you possess and the amazing number of places to which they can be delivered.

A *vulnerable area* means an area of the human body that will suffer an immediate painful and/or crippling reaction when attacked. Women usually respond to an attack by beating the assailant about the chest with the underside of their fists, which is like trying to stop a rhino with a BB gun. The wrong weapon is being used in the wrong area. Beating a man about the biceps with a stick will leave his arm sore and tender to the touch tomorrow morning, but it sure won't help you tonight! It is not a vulnerable area. However, poke that same stick into his eye or into his throat, hit him across the bridge of his nose or shins with it, or swing it upward into his groin area, and you have accomplished something, because any one of those areas will meet our definition: It will give an immediate painful or crippling reaction. (The best thing for you to do in the above emergency would be to hit him in all five areas mentioned, one after another. Why be half-safe?)

There are numerous vulnerable areas, but we will concentrate on those most applicable to your strength and probable skills. You will note that most of them are in the front of your body and a great number are concentrated in the head area. Let's start with the head.

Eyes. The most vulnerable area on the human body is the eye. We instinctively do more to protect our eyes than any other part of the body. And right here, let's start becoming realistic. The average woman, when I discuss this type of attack, wrinkles up her nose in distaste and says, "I just *couldn't* poke someone in the eye." Certainly the thought is repugnant, but so is the thought of your being raped, disfigured, violently injured, or killed. Don't lose sight of the fact that it was not you, but your attacker, knowing the consequences, who set it up. And always remember, you are probably not his first victim, and unless you are able to stop him, you won't be his last. I do *not* recommend attacking a man's eyes to stop him from forcing an unwanted kiss upon you at a party, but in a rape or violent assault, when you are in fear for your life or of grave bodily injury, it is not only morally, legally, and ethically justified, but absolutely necessary. Remember Barthol's Law!

Above all, understand that a halfway defense without surprise will invariably fail. You have to go all out and not worry about your opponent. He started it, not you, so control your natural compassion or you will lose. We live in the real world and must face it realistically. Violence is to be abhorred and avoided if possible, but if it is forced upon you, you have no choice. It is *your* life and limb at stake. Do what you have to do!

So, we use the eyes not only as a point of attack, but also for setting up surprise. A handful of outstretched fingers jabbed at an attacker's eyes will usually bring his guard up and set him up for attack in another area. And as you have seen dozens of times on TV, throw a handful of dirt, salt, whiskey, hot coffee—or cold coffee, for that matter—into his eyes. If it stings or burns, so much the better, but in any case, it will surprise him and cause him to back up or move his guard temporarily. Throw anything that is handy.

Nose. The average woman simply cannot slug hard enough to do much damage here, but the back or front of your head, an elbow, or your knee to the point of his nose, or a weapon, such

FIGURE 12–1.

as a heavy ash tray or a flashlight, across the bridge of his nose is very effective. Also, try this: Push hard with the side, not the fleshy tip, of your thumb in an *upward* and *inward* direction against the little bump of bone just under your nose and you will discover it to be very painful (Figure 12–1). We'll use this later.

Throat. This area, unprotected by either bones or muscles, is extremely vulnerable to a variety of attacks. A hard blow delivered here by a heavy object, particularly across the Adam's apple, will stop the hardiest male. Even a jabbing thumb can back him up. Pushing hard against the throat with the bone of your forearm or wrist can force his head back and thus push him off balance, set him up for a blow, or make him loosen a grip. Feel the hollow of your throat. Push your finger deeply into it in a downward direction—but gently (Figure 12–2). It hurts and will gag you. It will do the same to him, too.

FIGURE 12–2.

Ears. The ears are very sensitive to twisting, heavy, violent rubbing, and biting. In addition, "boxing" the ears, i.e., hitting them simultaneously with the cupped hands, creates a pressure within the ear that is extremely painful and could break the eardrums.

Mastoid process. Just behind your ear lobes you can feel a little hollow, right where the jawbone ends. Place the tips of your index fingers, or the ends of your thumbs, in that hollow and push inwardly and upward. You will feel some pain. This is difficult to feel on yourself, and to understand this area, you really have to try it on someone else and have it tried on you. Start rather gently because when the pain takes hold, *it takes hold*. This can be used to back someone away in a hurry (Figure 12–3).

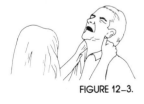

FIGURE 12–3.

Temple. This is a sensitive part of the head, and your extended knuckle's digging into this area will be painful enough to make him back up (Figure 12–4).

Hair. This is being included in the list of vulnerable areas because of its effectiveness for pulling someone off balance. Although having your hair pulled is a painful experience, it is hardly crippling, nor does it result in excruciating pain. How-

FIGURE 12–4.

ever, if the hair is pulled *correctly*, the result can be devastating. To accomplish this, the spread fingers should be slid upward through the back of the hair, then the grip closed in a twisting motion. This makes it next to impossible to pull the hair free. Then pull the hair *straight down the back*, not outward nor upward. This results in the head's being tilted back over the spine and the body bowed backward, hardly the classic on-balance position. With the body in this position, it is almost impossible to throw an effective blow or use your muscles effectively in any direction. We will find many uses for this later. So much for the head, a virtual treasure trove of vulnerable areas. But there are many more! Let's continue our inventory.

Trapezius muscle. Although this barely meets the definition of a vulnerable area, I'm including it here because it can be of great value to you under certain circumstances. This is the muscle that runs down the side of your neck and across the top of your shoulder. Reach over and feel it. Even better, get a grip on it and dig your thumb into it and pinch. Now do you see what I mean? When pinched, this muscle hurts! We can use this to make someone let go or to set him up for another attack as his attention is drawn to this spot.

Sternum. This is the breastbone, that bony structure between the bottom of your throat and the top of your stomach. I include it here for its one peculiar property: It is very painful when pushed hard by a pointed object. This move will not cripple anyone, but under less-than-lethal situations it has a definite value in making someone back up or let go. To find out about this, extend one knuckle and *push* (don't strike) it into the center of the breastbone of some willing colleague. I guarantee that he'll back up. This can be used against an amorous boyfriend or to move someone who is playfully blocking your way.

Solar plexus. This is the sensitive spot right below the bottom of your breastbone, where your ribs connect in the center of your body. Almost any hard blow here, particularly a penetrating one, will stop your attacker.

Back of the hand. This is a little-known and rarely used sensitive area that can be very vulnerable to you. Close your left

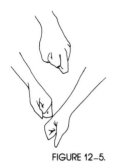

FIGURE 12-5.

hand into a tight fist. Extend the middle knuckle of your right hand and hit the back of your closed left hand sharply and hard with the *point* of that extended knuckle, right on or between the tendons (Figure 12–5). *Try it!* If you didn't cheat, it hurts. No damage is done, but it will make someone let go, and if the striking is made with a hard weapon, the blow will make it unlikely that he will want to use that hand for a few minutes. Better yet, beat a rapid and hard tattoo with the knuckles on *both* your hands. He might be able to stand one blow, but not a cumulative series of them!

Stomach and abdomen. Unless you are particularly strong and know how to deliver a blow like a man, your chances of stopping a robust male this way are remote, unless you use a heavy pointed object to jab into the area.

Groin. Here is the male's weakest spot. Any kind of a blow here is effective, subject to the problems of delivering it as discussed earlier. Just remember that a knee is only one of your many weapons. (We'll discuss this under "Personal Weapons.")

Knee, shin, anklebone. All of these are sensitive to kicks or blows with hard objects, because the bone is close to the skin, but usually a kick in the shins by a woman wearing ordinary light shoes will merely make the guy mad—or amused. A blow with a hard, heavy object (baseball bat, tire iron, flashlight, fireplace poker, soda bottle, frying pan, statue— the list is limited only by your imagination) on these areas will wipe the smile off his face.

FIGURE 12-6.

Toes and arch of foot. The average book always places much stock in having the attacked woman stomp on the man's toes or on top of the arch of his foot. Unless you have sharp high or very hard heels and he has light shoes, the results will probably be "eh-h-?"(Figure 12–6). Besides, it is usually a slow blow and you go off balance (on one foot) to deliver it, which makes *you* more vulnerable.

149

CHAPTER THIRTEEN

PERSONAL (NATURAL) WEAPONS

These are the natural weapons that can be formed by your body members, which are available to you in amazing abundance. You usually think of your arsenal as consisting of your fists, feet, knees, and maybe your teeth. Wait'll you take inventory!

Head. The main use of the head is for thinking, the best weapon ever created, but we also use it for butting, forward or backward (Figure 13–1).

FIGURE 13–1.

Teeth. I'll assume you know about biting.

Elbow. This is one of the most powerful weapons you own. You can deliver a rear-elbow blow with far more force than any other kind of blow, primarily because you will be able to put

153

more of your body behind it. (This is Principle 2, the use of all your muscles). *Try it!* Stand with your feet together, close your right fist, hold your forearm level with the floor, and without twisting your body, drive a blow straight back into the stomach of an imaginary attacker. I doubt that you would have wrinkled his T-shirt! (Figure 13–2). Now do the same thing again, but this time, do it right. Take a balanced position (legs shoulder-width apart, etc.), and then, bending your knees, twist your body to the left like a skier going into a left-hand turn, accomplishing the same thing as a baseball pitcher does in his wind-up, i.e., tightening the spring (Figure 13–3). Now you are ready. Suddenly unwind to the right, driving that elbow with the full power of your body, the power takeoff coming from your left leg (Figure 13–4). See the terrific power you can generate with this method compared with the first? This blow can be delivered to the stomach and abdomen. It is also extremely effective if administered to the groin, because that kind of a blow is unexpected and is easily as effective as if it were delivered by a knee. The rear-elbow blow is usually shown in most books as

FIGURE 13–2.

FIGURE 13–3.

FIGURE 13–4.

also being delivered to the neck and face, but that use is actually ineffective and I don't use it. The woman is usually shorter than her antagonist and therefore the blow has to be delivered upwards and close in. This puts your body in an awkward position, preventing you from using the principle that makes it so powerful, the use of all your muscles. *Try it!*

Forearm. The forearm can be used for what the wrestlers term a "forearm smash," a dramatic term, but quite accurate. The bone of your forearm, between the wrist and elbow, is driven with as much force as possible to the face or throat of your adversary (Figure 13–5). To get this force, it must be delivered

FIGURE 13–5.

with all your muscles behind it. (A basic rule in delivering this or any other blow is to try to bury it into your opponent. Don't just make contact and quit; follow through and try to make it come out the other side of your target.)

FIGURE 13–6.

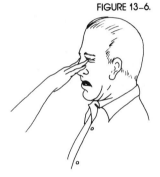

Hands. These are the most versatile weapons we own. Let's subdivide the hands and see what we have:

OPEN HAND. The fingers are extended and spread and used for jabbing at the eyes (Figure 13–6).

OPEN HAND. The fingers are extended but held tightly together. Jab into the throat or solar plexus.

OPEN HAND. *Probably the most deadly attack in your entire repertoire is the grasping hand to the groin.* Whether your arms are free or pinned to your sides, or whether you are standing, sitting, or rolling on the ground, you usually have a pretty good chance to use this. Grab his testicles, squeeze as hard as you can, and twist. This is not playing by the rules but, in a real life-or-death assault, is *quite probably the only thing you can do that will save you,* and that is what this book is all about. Because it is so deadly, so unexpected, so effective, and so hard to defend against, this tactic will be used later as our principal weapon against the male of the species. Again, I repeat: it is probably the *only* effective technique you have under many circumstances.

SINGLE FINGER. Use it for poking (into the eye, under the jaw, into the mastoid process, up into the nose) and pulling (inside the corner of the mouth).

FIST. Use it to deliver blows, primarily to the nose or groin.

TOP OR BOTTOM OF FIST. These can administer hammer-type blows to the nose, solar plexus, or groin (Figure 13–7).

FIGURE 13–7.

Remember that in a real-life attack you won't always be standing on your two feet facing your opponent. You may be upside-down, crossways, on the ground, in the process of being dragged face up or face down, or in any combination of these or other positions, and the standard weapons and the standard method of delivery may not be practical. Therefore, the top or bottom of the fist delivered in a hammer-blow fashion may be the only practical weapon.

SINGLE EXTENDED KNUCKLE. This can be used for delivering blows to the temple or to the back of the hand or pressure on the breastbone.

HEEL OF THE HAND. Here is another surprisingly efficient weapon. The heel of the hand is the bottom part of your open palm, the heavy bone structure that runs horizontally from the base of the thumb across to the little-finger side. The heel-of-the-hand blow is particularly effective because you can get all your body power behind it against vulnerable areas just made for this weapon. It is used against the nose or chin (Figure 13–8) to drive the attacker back and away from you or even to stun him, and against the inside of the wrist to break his grip or move his arm to the side.

FIGURE 13–8.

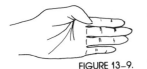

FIGURE 13-9.

EDGE OF THE HAND. This is simply the outside, or little-finger side, of the stiff open hand and is used to deliver the "judo chop." The hand is held stiffly, fingers straight and together, thumb touching the index finger and never extended outward, the wrist straight, and the hand very slightly cupped (Figure 13–9). The blow is struck with the fleshy part of the edge of the hand between the base of the little finger and the bone at the bottom of the hand. The blow should be struck cross-body, or backhand, as this is the only way you can get all your muscles behind it (Figure 13–10). It can also be used to strike a downward blow. This is a versatile, jack-of-all-trades weapon, used against almost any vulnerable area not consisting of bone (such as the shin). It is particularly well suited for use against the bridge of the nose and the throat, neck, and groin. Another unexpected blow (the principle of surprise again) is the chop to the groin that can be delivered to the rear when your arms are either free or pinned (Figure 13–11), as we will discuss in detail later under "Body Locks."

FIGURE 13-10.

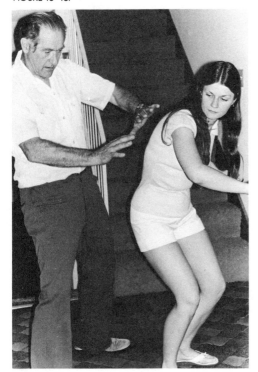

FIGURE 13-11.

Knee. Deliver blows to the groin and abdominal areas and face, if close enough.

Feet. Here is another versatile weapon we can subdivide:

TOE. Kick into shins. This is not very effective unless you have heavy shoes (or very strong toes).

HEEL. Stomp on his toes. This is usually when he is behind you. Again, it's not very effective unless you have hard heels or he is barefoot.

BALL OF FOOT. Stomp on his toes or arch.

EDGE OF FOOT. This really should read "edge of shoes," because it means scraping the outside edge of the hard sole of your shoe up and down his shin bone. Without shoes this could be called "massage," hardly a deadly weapon.

CHAPTER FOURTEEN

PHYSICAL SELF-DEFENSE TECHNIQUES

To those of you who immediately turned to this chapter without reading those that go before it, I can only tell you that, without the knowledge set forth in Chapters 11 through 13, these techniques will not work properly and may not work at all. If you wanted to plant a lawn and bought the finest grass seeds but then merely tossed them out on unprepared ground, you would get at best a few patchy spots of weak grass, or maybe nothing at all. Why? No preparation. If, on the other hand, you thoroughly prepared the ground, added the right fertilizers, planted the grass carefully and evenly, and thereafter watered it, the chances are that you would have a full, rich lawn. This chapter and the succeeding ones are merely the seeds. The preceding chapters contain the instructions for preparing the ground. If you are serious about self-defense, go back and read those chapters. It could mean your life.

Of course, prevention is the best technique; talking your way out of the situation is next best. Physical contact is the last resort. The following techniques are for use when there is nothing else left. These techniques look and are simple to perform. Each one has been researched over and over again under combat conditions, and they do work. I'm leaving out dozens of techniques usually shown in other self-defense courses because experience has shown that they work fine in a gym with a cooperative partner but fail in combat on the streets. Most fail because they are better suited to a trained boxer or karate or judo expert than they are to the average untrained person. Also, a few good, well-learned techniques are better than a hundred partly learned methods.

Physical training is the foundation of this or any other kind of defense, and any training, particularly in gymnastics or judo, in which you learn the basic principles mentioned earlier, will stand you in good stead now. In fact, training in any of the self-defense arts will help you. While judo and other like arts reduce the importance of the element of strength as a deciding factor in combat, the stronger you are, the better. Fitness and training are vital.

Now, at last, to the physical techniques. *Caution:* They have been carefully analyzed, with all extra or showy movements eliminated, leaving only the necessary elements. Please don't try to add to or subtract from them. You may have previously learned some technique that is similar, but not *identical* to mine. It is therefore not the same. Learn mine the way I have set them out—*exactly* as they have been set out. If you don't, they won't work as well *and may not work at all.* (It is not that you can't use other techniques—there *are* other good methods—it's just that my particular techniques work best the way I have set them out.)

In reading books and articles in this field over the years, I have been struck by the consistent lack of detailed instructions on the finer points of the techniques taught. The description of the techniques and photographs illustrating the major moves are there, but that is all. To become proficient—in fact, to make the techniques work at all—you must also be taught how, when, and where to apply leverage, the exact positioning of your body to bring into play all the basic principles (which usually nobody explains in the first place), the methods of setting up surprise, and many other points the reader may not know exist. Most books don't cover these points, and the inexperienced reader can't even use guesswork, because she doesn't know that something is missing.

One reason for this lack is that the authors are afraid the book will be too long and that the reader will get bored with long, detailed explanations. This may be true, but why bother at all if your work will be merely exercise, with little chance that it will work under actual emergency conditions? The tragedy is that the trusting readers may believe in the effectiveness of the teaching, and that could cost them their lives if they tried the techniques and they failed to work. When I first started teaching these techniques to law-enforcement officers, I suddenly realized that they were trusting their very lives to my teachings. What an awesome responsibility that placed on me! I decided right then and there that what I taught would always be honest, and, before I taught it, it would be researched under combat conditions so that any weaknesses of each technique would be pointed out. Any method that failed under stress would no longer be taught. So bear with the long and detailed instructions. Pay close attention to the warnings and cautions included, usually signalled by *italics*. Believe me when I tell you how and how not to practice. I may lose readers because they feel it isn't worth the trouble to wade through all this, but those who do will have an honest presentation of techniques that *will* work if they are learned properly.

Before the actual physical contact, there are a few general suggestions that will help immeasurably in your learning. First, your choice of a partner. One of the hardest things to find is someone to practice with (or on). I strongly suggest that you choose another woman. The reasons for not choosing a male for this have been abundantly demonstrated over the years I have been teaching. The male ego becomes involved, no matter how hard he tries to submerge it. You will try to work a technique on your male and he will instinctively resist you, at the time when you are just learning. The technique won't work and you will become discouraged and lose interest. *I have seen more women turned away from these studies because of this than for any other reason.* Believe me. Get another woman, preferably one who is as interested as you are, and take turns practicing the methods covered in this book. Even better, get a group of women together.

Pitfalls in learning

Another common and extremely discouraging mistake is to try the new techniques (which you really have not yet mastered) on your husband, boyfriend, brother, or male friend. First, you are obviously *not* going to go all out against your friendly male, and most of these techniques work *only* if you put everything you have behind them. Second, the male ego is again involved (*he* isn't going to be beaten by a girl!). Third, you undoubtedly removed the element of surprise, the one thing necessary to make it work, by telling him, "Let me show you what I learned! Try to strangle me." The result? He will easily block your move and then overpower you (because you have no surprise, you don't have it completely learned, and you are not going all out).

One problem you will have in practicing these techniques is that the instructions are very long and detailed, and it is very difficult to be going through each step and have to break off to read the next step or be sure you got the current step right. Here is where a third partner could really help. *Be sure you read the entire set of instructions on a given technique all the way through before you attempt even the first step.* Then, while you are working with your partner, have the third partner read the instructions to you step by step. She can even correct your errors as you progress. Then take turns until you all have had a crack at it. I think that this is the best way to learn. Resolve right now to be patient and cover every step thoroughly. It will pay off by enabling you to really become adept at the art of self-defense.

Don't try to go too fast. Don't try to learn everything in one session. Don't quit and go on to something else if one technique doesn't seem to work. Keep plugging. They all work! One of the worst pitfalls is the compulsion to move too fast. Learn each method step by step, preferably in slow motion at first. *Speed is your enemy!* By moving fast, you develop sloppy moves and your chances of learning correctly are very poor. By practicing each technique very slowly, you can catch any wrong moves and correct them. You will be setting up a habit in your brain, a conditioned reflex. When an actual emergency does come, speed will be there! You can move awfully fast if you are scared. But when you do have to move, your habit-patterns will take over, and you will do it correctly. And it will work.

However, to be sure it will work in an emergency, you must practice, practice, and practice until you have engraved the moves permanently onto your brain. And here's a nice surprise: You can effectively practice the techniques in slow motion. After you have thoroughly learned them, get together with your partner (or somebody else) occasionally and just walk through the moves to keep them fresh in your mind and reinforce the patterns. Knocking each other around at full combat speed isn't necessary. I do suggest, however, that you practice the less-lethal techniques on a willing male friend, but only after you have learned them *thoroughly.* Two hours of practice before trying them on a male just isn't enough. You'll end up being discouraged, as discussed above. Also, remember that if there is no surprise, the chances that *anything* will work is small. I do expect you to have fun learning the techniques, but don't get too rough or engage in a lot of horseplay or someone may be injured. If your partner makes fast moves to show how she can block you during practice, get another partner. We're here to learn. The enemy is too much speed at first. Remember that!

Don't get discouraged at first when you can't put the various moves together smoothly and without long thought. Let me remind you of when you began to drive a car, particularly if you learned on a car with a stick shift. You learned to steer accurately, learned to let the clutch out slowly, learned to shift smoothly, learned to increase the gas slowly, learned to give a hand signal, and learned to check the rear-view mirror for cars overtaking you. All easy. But notice that I put "learned to" before each skill. I did that because that is the way you learned each skill—separately. The catch came when you had to put every one of these things together quickly into one smooth, continuous operation. Remember what happened? You buck-jumped the car down the street, killed the motor, forgot to check the rear-view mirror and give the hand signal, ground the gears horrendously, and probably almost hit the curb. You felt then that you could never get it together and you would always be a bus rider. Now, you can do all these things while driving uphill and around a curve in heavy traffic, without missing a word of conversation with your passengers, and not even be aware of what you're doing! Why? Practice, practice, practice, first slowly, and then at normal speeds. Notice that you didn't practice driving a car at emergency speeds, but that now, when emergencies come, you can whip into the routines without conscious thought and do them smoothly. The same thing will happen in your self-defense techniques. Learn them slowly and thoroughly and practice regularly, and they will be there without conscious thought when you need them. Trust me!

COUNTERS AND ESCAPE TECHNIQUES

As a verb, *to counter* means "to oppose." I'm using it here as a noun, to give a name to any technique used to oppose an action by your opponent; for example, a *counter* to a choke. The counters you will learn here are actually used as escape techniques.

The rest of this book describes counters developed against the more common forms of assaults made on women. As you will notice, they are surprisingly simple. Any technique that requires that you be a combination acrobat and gymnast to execute it is utterly useless. The ones shown here can be executed by anyone with normal coordination. All you have to do is learn them correctly and execute them with surprise. We'll start with one that looks simple, but that requires a lot of little fine points applied correctly to make it effective. The effort is worth it. Here is where you learn to follow my instructions to the letter. Important: *Read through each counter completely without any physical involvement before starting the step-by-step learning.*

COUNTERS TO WRIST GRASPS

There is no one among you who has not had some male grab her by the wrist to hold her or drag her someplace she doesn't want to go. It is one of the most common assaults on women. Mere struggling, pulling, or jerking is not going to break you loose. However, the following counter, well-learned and executed with surprise, will leave the grabber wondering where you went. This counter can be used in all sorts of situations, from the one in which the rapist is attempting to drag you off into some nice shrubbery to the one in which your boyfriend is dragging you to the edge of the pool to throw you in.

169

Start by facing your partner. Stick out your right arm as if you intended to shake hands. Your partner will shake hands with the *inside of your wrist* with her right hand (Figure 15–1). Now consider Principle 3: Attack your opponent's weakest spot. (Note: If you skipped over the chapter on basic principles, you will be lost. Stop. Go back and read it now. We'll wait for you.) Look at her grip on your wrist: The strongest part (her four fingers) is on the lower or little-finger side of your wrist, and the weak part (her thumb) is on the upper or thumb side of your wrist. You are going to jerk your wrist up hard and fast *against her thumb*, the weak part of her grip. (Be sure you are both using your right hands, and, partner, remember that there is no surprise here, so hold the wrist firmly but not too tightly while we learn.) *Try it!*

It may or may not have worked. But now let's add in the fine points, like Principle 1, balance. Bend your knees and your wrist slightly, and twist your body slightly to the left, like a skier's left-turn stance. This winds up and cocks the spring (Figure 15–2). Remember Principle 2, the use of *all* your muscles? When you go into action, close your right fist and unwind suddenly, letting loose the springs you cocked. Drive off that left leg. (Remember the power-line?) Jerk the arm upward; don't merely pull it. Principle 3, attack the weakest spot: Be sure your upward jerk is directly against that thumb, not a sideward sweep. *Try it!*

It should have worked much better, but did you throw yourself off balance as you came up, leaning over backward as in Figure 15–3? Probably. Almost all beginners do. This leaves you off balance and therefore very vulnerable to a counterattack. So let's correct this and add a couple more of the fine points to your technique. This time, as you jerk your arm upward, try to hit your right shoulder with your fist. You can't, but come as close to it as possible. And, most important, at the same time throw your elbow *violently* forward as if you were going to bury it in an attacker's solar plexus. You won't actually hit him with the elbow, but the motion does two things: It adds a great deal more leverage against his thumb, and by aiming at his solar plexus you keep your elbow in the same line as your moving hand. If your elbow sticks out like a chicken wing, you've lost a great deal of leverage, and leverage is what makes

FIGURE 15–1.

FIGURE 15–2.

FIGURE 15–3.

this work. So keep your fist and elbow in that straight line as your elbow drives toward his midsection and your fist toward your own shoulder. *Try it!*

Now we'll add the final touch: As you jerk upward, bend your waist slightly and step forward with your left foot *directly into your opponent,* all in one smooth motion (Figure 15–4). When, after practice, you get it right, you'll find your partner (or opponent) is forced backward and off balance, while you are ready to step forward with your right knee to the groin and a forearm smash to the throat or a heel of the hand to the nose (Figure 15–5) or merely turn and run. *Try it!* Several times! It should start working about now.

FIGURE 15–4.

FIGURE 15–5.

Now we'll try a variation. Raise your *right* forearm as if you were thumbing your nose at your partner, who will grab your wrist with her *right* hand (Figure 15–6). Note that the strong side of her grip (her four fingers) is now on the upper or thumb side of your wrist, and the weak spot (her thumb) is on the bottom or little-finger side of your wrist. So, if you jerked upward, it would. be against the strongest spot of her grip, the four fingers. Instead, we jerk *downward. Try it!* (Be sure the jerk was downward, not sideward.) Did you get on balance? Use all your muscles? Try it again, but this time, as you jerk downward, bend at the knees and waist, twist your body slightly to the right, and jerk your right fist past and close to the outside of your right knee (Figure 15–7). (Don't go more than a couple of inches past it.) *Try it!* For a follow-through, *immediately* whip the *top* of your right fist back up into his groin (Figure 15–8). This counter-attack must be immediate and as fast as you possibly can do it, or he'll block it. Surprise is everything.

Now let's really make it difficult. Stick out your right hand as if you were shaking hands again, but this time your partner will grab your wrist with *both* her hands (Figure 15–9). Take a good look. Note that the strong part of her grip (eight fingers) is underneath, and you are looking at the weak spot, her two thumbs. First, never give the other guy any advantage. She has two hands working; you only have one. Okay: Close your right fist, then reach over with your left hand *between* her arms, over your own right fist, and grab the fist. Now we are even—two arms each! Get set—balanced (Figure 15–10)—and *with every muscle in your body,* you're going to jerk upward against her

FIGURE 15–6.

FIGURE 15–7.

FIGURE 15–8.

FIGURE 15–9.   FIGURE 15–10.

two thumbs. *Be sure to throw that right elbow to her solar plexus and jerk your right fist to your right shoulder. Try it!*

Now add the fine points: As you jerk upward, bend forward at the waist and step *forward*, directly into your partner, again putting it all together in one smooth motion. You should look like the woman shown in Figure 15–11 when this move is completed. Do you? Ask your partner!

You can follow through by stepping forward again with the right leg, driving your knee to the groin and a right forearm smash to the throat, or a heel of the hand to the nose (Figure 15–12).

FIGURE 15–11.   FIGURE 15–12.

FIGURE 15-13.

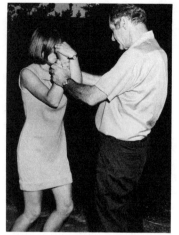

FIGURE 15-14.

Now learn the two-handed counter, used when your arm is up and your partner grabs it two-handed from underneath (Figure 15–13). We use the same technique, except this time you reach *under* your own arm, between her arms, and grab your fist (Figure 15–14). This time jerk *downward* (Figure 15–15). Follow through with the top of your fist to the groin (Figure 15–16).

Now that you've learned the basic wrist-grasp counters, I'm going to change the rules slightly. You learned the one-hand counter to a one-hand wrist grasp (Figures 15–1 through 15–8), a vital technique. However, some of you may have wondered why Principle 2, the use of all your muscles, doesn't play a part in that counter. It does, it does! (We're talking about why your

FIGURE 15-15.

FIGURE 15-16.

FIGURE 15-17.

other hand was not put into play in the counter.) We learned the one-hand counter first because there are times when your second hand can't be brought into play, and you need this skill. Your opponent may have grabbed both of your wrists, for example, or you may have something in your other hand, like your purse, or you are holding on to your car door to keep from being dragged away. There are many reasons. However, when you can, you will use *both* hands in every instance. The *two-handed* counter to the *one-hand* wrist grasp is much more effective, as it helps equalize the usual advantage of size and strength that the male has.

To use this new counter, you have nothing new to learn. Simply add the other hand to your closed fist exactly as you do for the two-handed-grasp counter (Figure 15–17). Simple, isn't it? Please, however, practice the one-hand counter also. It will be *very* necessary on occasion, and if you learn to do it effectively with one hand, think how devastating you'll be with two!

Now start practicing all possible combinations (your attacker won't always grab your right wrist with his right hand): Have your partner grab your right wrist, first with her left, then her right hand; then your left wrist with her right and then her left hand; then learn the two-handed counter when she grabs your left wrist. Keep practicing the various combinations, but slowly. Speed will come when you need it!

Review: The two most common errors are:

1. Failure to thrust the elbow forward and in a straight line toward the assailant's solar plexus.
2. Bending over backward as you jerk up instead of stepping *into* your opponent.

Now add a combat technique that is *absolutely vital*. The natural instinct for a man or woman is to make a panic move when attacked, with the excellent possibility that the move will be wrong. Instead, when the attack comes, hesitate just a moment *to take a look at the situation*. In the wrist grasp, take a quick moment to decide where the thumb is so you know which way to jerk, and also to collect your thoughts so that the move is effective. The time spent (a second or less) may make the difference between success or failure. We can ensure success by how we practice. *After* you have learned the techniques thoroughly (don't rush this), have your partner grab you in various ways suddenly, and react as fast as you can to get away. You will see very quickly what I mean and learn to take that extra second. *This practice is vital. It is part of the necessary stress training.*

COUNTER TO GRASPING HANDS (FINGER PEELBACK)

This counter is an all-purpose little dandy that will come in handy in all sorts of situations, from the one in which you deal with a rapist to the one in which you encounter an overamorous clutching drunk at a family party. It will enable you to quickly and quietly remove a hand from wherever it is to some better place of your own choosing, with great pain to the owner of the hand, if you so choose to inflict it.

This will work with his thumb, little finger (always the best because it is the weakest), or any finger that seems the most available.

1. Have your partner stand behind you and wrap her arms around your waist, grasping her left wrist with her right hand.

2. Using your opposite hand (in this case, your left) to her top hand, dig your four fingers under either the thumb or the little finger, whichever appears to be the most available. (Partner: Make it easy the first few times until she gets the hang of it.) Take a *full* grip on the finger after you pry it up, and bend it back toward the top of her wrist as far as possible (Figure 15–18).

3. Maintaining your grip, whirl your body to the outside, and as you come face to face, your partner should be bending backward with slightly bent knees to relieve the pain (Figures 15–19 and 15–20).

FIGURE 15–18.

FIGURE 15–19.

FIGURE 15–20.

FIGURE 15–21.

4. By straightening out your arm toward your own feet, and adding as much more bend to her finger as possible, you can bring her to her knees (Figure 15–21). If the real-life situation warrants it, bring your inside knee up into your attacker's strategically placed groin and/or the heel of your hand up under his nose.

If the finger available is difficult to get hold of, use the other hand to assist in prying it loose. One fact to keep in mind is that he can resist your strength for a short period, but the unrelenting power of *all your muscles* against his poor little pinkie will prevail. All of a sudden he will run out of strength and the finger will come loose. He can't help it; he'll just run out of steam, so don't give up. Keep prying. When it does come loose, get your firm grip on it and continue as above.

COUNTERS TO HAND CHOKES

Before you get into the actual counters, you should have a little background information concerning the subject. Throughout history, one of the most common attack techniques has been the strangle, or as it is usually called, the choke. This should be of particular interest to women, because the choke is the favorite of the rapist, prowler, and attackers in general. And for a good reason: By cutting off the woman's breath, he has also choked off her screams, and, in a very few moments, eliminated any resistance. Unlike most other forms of violence, this one can control the degree of harm rather precisely by deciding when to release his hold. He can merely frighten her, choke her into temporary unconsciousness, or continue until death. Untold thousands of victims would be alive today if they had only known the simple counters to a strangle. Before we go into the defensive techniques, you should understand what a strangle is and what it is not. If a strangler merely cuts off your air, you can live and resist for a relatively long period of time. How long? How long can you hold your breath? A minute? Two minutes? Some can hold out as long as three minutes. The poor guy would get bored and lose interest if all his victims took that long to succumb! However, if he squeezes the carotid arteries, which run up each side of your neck and supply the blood to the brain, he has cut off that blood supply, and your survival time is drastically reduced, because you will become unconscious in seconds, even though you might still have plenty of air left in your lungs.

This brings us to the most important rule there is concerning strangles. *No method is worth a damn unless it is designed to remove the choking hands or arms from your throat within about three seconds.* I have read many articles and texts advocating a thrust to the eyes, a knee to the groin, a chop to the kidneys, or the like, as fine methods of countering a choke. But if you failed to really disable your attacker with the first few tries, *it is too late!* The chances are that you will become woozy in a few seconds, and even if you are still conscious, your struggles will be just that—aimless struggles, without any coherent and intelligently directed plan. The chances of your hitting a determined male in the eye or groin (about the only vulnerable areas that might give fast enough reactions for your survival) are rather slim, because of your awkward position and because he's expecting that kind of attack.

Before we proceed further, I must convince you once and for all that most methods advocated for all these years as counters to choke holds are dishonest, because they simply won't work for the average female - or male, for that matter. Go to somebody else's books or other "experts" and learn the "slap-off," the "peel-off," the "flying wedge," and numerous other maneuvers, and the various chops, pokes, and gouges that they recommend. Then, working with a cooperative male friend, try them, and see if you can get loose in three seconds—or at all! Have him *really* hold you. (He doesn't have to actually choke you. Holding his hands rigidly around your throat will do the job.) These methods *might* work in the hands of a trained expert, but usually work only in a gym with a cooperative partner who doesn't really dig in. *Try it!* I must convince you so that you will learn only techniques that I know will work, even when used by a small woman. Strangles come in various sizes and shapes. There are arm strangles and hand strangles, from the front and rear, standing, kneeling, and prone. No one counter works for all, but all effective counters have one thing in common—they get those unwanted hands off your throat in about three seconds.

We'll start with the counter to the simplest of the chokes, the standing, face-to-face, two-hand strangle from the front. This counter is the only one that comes with an iron-clad guarantee. It will work, even when applied by a small woman against a large, chauvinistic male. I call this method the "windmill" counter, because that term is descriptive. It looks very simple, but don't be fooled! Unless you learn it slowly and correctly *exactly as set out,* it may not work. Why? Because its success depends entirely upon the leverage applied in exactly the right way. If you change or omit any of the instructions, you probably won't have enough leverage to make it work. So let's try it.

Counter to a standing front choke

Have your partner face you and take a gentle but firm two-handed-choke grip on your throat. The following instructions, although broken down into steps to learn, are actually executed in one smooth motion. *It should be learned in slow motion.*

1. First, as you face your partner, the wall in front of you is the front wall. Now locate and remember the left- and right-hand walls and the back wall. These are necessary for your later orientation.

2. Swing your *straight* right arm in a half circle to the outside (like drawing a line up that right-hand wall) until your arm is pointing straight to the sky (Figure 15–22).

3. While you pivot or spin on the ball of your left foot, twist your upper body to the left so that it is facing the left-hand wall; at the same time, continue the swing of your right arm until it is pointing at the same left-hand wall, lying straight across her two choking arms (Figure 15–23). Note: Your arm is still straight and *rigid. It must be rigid.*

4. Continue to swing your right leg around until you have executed a *complete* about-face (you should now be directly facing the back wall), and at the same time continuing the sweep of that straight and *rigid* right arm around and down until your open hand slaps your right thigh *hard* (Figure 15–24). This is the key to this counter: Keep the right arm straight and *rigid* all the way and slap the thigh hard. *If you don't do these two things, the counter may not work.* I will repeat this: *If you don't keep the swinging arm straight and rigid all the way and slap your thigh hard, it may not work.* Have your partner tell you if you are doing it right. The reason for these absolutes is that the counter depends on the nutcracker-like leverage of your action at your armpit, with your body being one arm of the nutcracker and your swinging arm the other. If one arm of your nutcracker were flexible, it wouldn't work. Neither would this

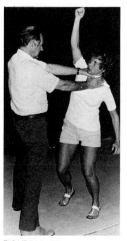

FIGURE 15–22.   FIGURE 15–23.

counter work with a flexible arm. We slap the thigh hard because this forces you to complete the swing and do it fast, which is what gives us that last bit of leverage that assures its success. Trust me!

5. You have now peeled the two hands off your throat. They may simply be gone, or they may be temporarily trapped under your right armpit, as shown in Figure 15–24.

6. Immediately step straight backward with your left leg and strike a bottom-of-the-fist blow or a judo chop to the groin (Figure 15–25) or grab his groin with your left hand and twist.

7. Now try the whole maneuver several times *all by yourself* (without your partner) until you get the about-face and the swinging arm together in one smooth motion. Your partner can

FIGURE 15–24.   FIGURE 15–25.

help by correcting anything you are doing wrong—particularly the straightness of your arm. And I'll bet she didn't hear the slap. If she couldn't hear, you are not doing it right!

8. Now work it a few more times with your partner choking you until you learn to do it smoothly. Have her increase her grip as tight as you can stand it (the secret in practice is to have a rigid grip without digging the thumb and fingers into the throat) until you learn to react fast and effectively.

Review: the most common errors are:

1. Failure to keep the swinging arm straight and rigid.
2. Failure to slap your thigh with the straight-arm hand.
3. Failure to make the arm-swing and body-turn one smooth, continuous movement.

After you have mastered this counter thoroughly, practice your combat technique. Have your partner really come on strong with the strangle, and react as fast as you can. You will probably louse it up the first couple of times, but that is why we practice under combat conditions. Keep at it until it works every time. Remember that split-second hesitation we used under wrist grasps to size up the situation and think your move first. *This is a must!*

Counter to a rear hand-choke

A variation of the standing two-handed choke is the one in which the assailant is choking you from the rear. It is an inefficient choke, but some of our attackers are rather inept. (They just don't make attackers like they used to!) This will be easy, because you have already learned the counter—the "windmill." This will be the exact reverse of what we did in the front choke. We're going to use the same swinging "windmill" arm, but backward. In many ways this variation is easier to handle than the front standing choke, because you end up facing the attacker with his vulnerable areas more open to attack.

1. Have your partner stand behind you and take a two-handed grip on the back of your neck (Figure 15–26).

FIGURE 15–26.   FIGURE 15–27.

2. Just as you start your action, bend your neck to your left, trapping her hand momentarily. This will "squish" her grip and make her less able to hold you.

3. Now we do two things simultaneously: Pivoting on your *left* foot, whirl to your left, and at the same time swing your *left* arm up and behind you, straight and rigid as before (Figure 15–27).

4. Complete your whirling turn to a complete about-face, until you are directly facing her, and complete the swinging arm motion up and around until you slap your thigh (Figure 15–28). You now should have peeled her hands off your throat, probably trapping them under your arms momentarily.

5. Now the obvious—jam the heel of the hand to the nose or chin and knee to the groin (Figure 15–29) or a right-handed grasp to the groin.

FIGURE 15–28.   FIGURE 15–29.

Counter to a kneeling choke

Another choking position is one in which the attacker is standing and the victim is on her knees in front of him. This comes about when the choke starts face to face but the victim is driven to or falls upon her knees. You and your partner take this position, her hands upon your throat (Figure 15–30).

1. With your right arm, swing up and over her choking hands with the same windmill counter we described before, twisting your body as far as you can to the left (Figure 15–31). This will break the choke from your throat.

FIGURE 15–30.

FIGURE 15–31.

FIGURE 15–32.

FIGURE 15–33.

2. Suddenly reverse your direction, twisting to the right and following through with a left-hand grasp to the groin (Figure 15–32).

3. Maintaining your grasp (squeeze!), strike as hard as you can with your right fist or extended knuckles to the throat (Figure 15–33).

This three-step attack is necessary, because your ending position has you off balance and very vulnerable to the next attack. Practice it a number of times until you feel the rhythm and balance of it. You will find that you can strike effective blows while you are on your knees.

4. Of course, as soon as you can, *take off!* Always leave the immediate vicinity of the attack and go for help or safety. Your attacker is not a fellow you would enjoy chatting with anyway.

Counter to a floor choke (straddle)

Up to now we have been talking about a face-to-face choke in which you were on your feet. In real life, chokes usually end up in a horizontal position on the ground, and many of them start there. It is easy to break the strangle with the windmill while you are on your feet, but it's not so easy if you are on the ground (or on your bed).

If you are being strangled on the ground, the strangler is either straddling you, with his knees on either side of your body, or he is kneeling alongside you, with both knees on one side of your body. In either case, his position has a fatal weakness that we can take advantage of. We will apply the principle of balance *against him*, because in both these positions, he will be leaning forward to get the necessary pressure on your throat. This means he is overbalanced forward and the only thing that keeps him from falling on his face is his two straight arms supported on your throat. We are going to help him go completely off balance with the right kind of shove. (After all, it *is* an uncomfortable position!)

First, lie on your back and have your partner straddle you, grasping your throat with both hands. (For the purpose of instruction, I'll specify the right or left leg, etc. In real life you use whichever seems best at the time.)

1. Cock your left leg, putting your foot *flat* on the floor, your thigh against her buttocks (Figure 15–34). That flat foot is the anchor for your power takeoff.

2. Drive your two arms forward, parallel to the floor, striking as close to her wrists as you can with the web of your hands (the web is the V formed between your outstretched thumb and pointer finger), with your thumbs on the inside and your fingers on the outside of her wrists (Figure 15–35). Try to drive her arms past and over your head. (Practice steps 2 and 3 separately and slowly a couple of times before you put them together.)

3. *At the same time,* kick as hard as you can and as far as you can with your cocked right leg, as if you were trying to drive her through the far wall. Use that anchored left leg as your power takeoff. This brings your thigh in sudden contact with her buttocks (don't worry; it won't hurt her, no matter how hard you kick). Remember, *the hand blows and the kick must be simultaneous* (Figure 15–36). Your partner will be pitched forward over your head, because she was already overbalanced in that direction and you removed the props (her two arms) and gave her a helpful push in that direction.

4. As she pitches forward, *immediately* twist your body *violently* to your right, pushing off that left foot (power line), carrying her two arms with you (Figure 15–37).

5. You will probably end up on your right side, lying across her left leg. You may not be clear of her, but *the choke has been broken,* which is exactly what we set out to do, and broken within the prescribed three seconds. Now you have to refer to the discussions of the personal weapons and of the vulnerable areas and use whatever you can depending on exactly how you ended up. A fingers-jab to the eyes (Figure 15–38), the edge of your forearm into his groin, your sharp elbow dug into his solar plexus, a heel of the hand under the nose—all these are good, but always remember the best, the grasp to the groin. Let go with your left hand and come up under the groin area with a scooping motion and grasp hard! *This is no game!* If the situation is serious, you must hurt your opponent badly and even incapacitate him or he will merely grab you again and start

FIGURE 15–34.

FIGURE 15–35.

FIGURE 15–36.

FIGURE 15–37.

FIGURE 15–38.

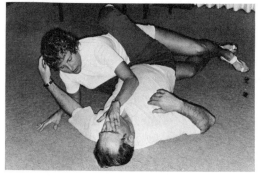

all over, probably with much more violence to you. If you are outdoors, a handful of dirt or sand thrown into his eyes is very effective. (If you are not a neat housekeeper, this might be available indoors . . . .)

6. Then get away—*now!* Don't even wait for a backward glance. *Take off!*

Counter to a floor choke (alongside)

We'll teach this counter in two parts: first, the leg motions, then the arm motions. Lie on your back, and this time your partner will kneel alongside you on your *left* side, her hands grasping your throat. (In real life, the attacker will be leaning forward with his weight on his two arms, so practice it this way.)

1. Cock your right leg, foot flat on the floor (Figure 15–39).

2. Draw your left leg up, as high as possible, to your chest (Figure 15–40).

3. Turn slightly to your left and insert your bent left leg between you and your partner with your left shin (not your knee) jammed against her waistline (Figure 15–41).

4. Thrust forward violently with your left leg, shoving her backward over her own heels, and probably breaking the choke (Figure 15–42). The force necessary for this comes from the pressure of your right foot against the floor, and your buttocks will be lifted off the ground as you arch your back and push off from your shoulders. You have tremendous strength in your thigh muscles, and with the leverage you have from this position you can dislodge your opponent.

To make certain this works, we will add some hand and arm motions. We will start as before, on your back, partner kneeling alongside, hands on your throat. Don't use any leg motions yet. As an aid to learning the arm motions, stretch your left arm over your head along the floor and your right arm down along your right side. (This is only an aid to learning; we do *not* do it in combat.)

5. Bring your left forearm down and place it at the break of her right elbow as close to your own elbow as possible.

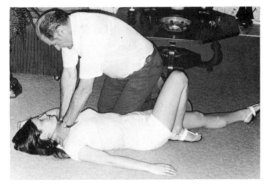

FIGURE 15-39.

FIGURE 15-40.

FIGURE 15-41.

FIGURE 15-42.

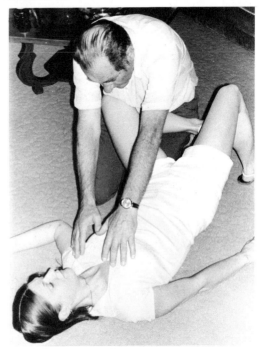

6. Come up with the heel of your right hand, placing it on the outside of her left elbow. You now look like the woman shown in Figure 15–43.

7. Practice the two arm motions separately. First, the left: Drive downward with your left forearm, trying to jam her elbow *inward* into the middle of your stomach. Practice this several times.

8. Now your right, again separately: With the heel of your right hand, jam her elbow *upward* and across your body. Try it a few times.

9. Next, put the two hand motions together and practice them a few times without any leg motions until you can get them working simultaneously and smoothly (Figure 15–44).

10. Now we put them all together. Have your partner kneel along your left side and take the choke hold. Execute all the *preliminary* motions (steps 1, 2, 3, 5, and 6). *You are not ready to break the choke until you are in this preparatory position.* Now go into the leg thrust and the arm motions simultaneously, making it one smooth motion (Figure 15–45). *To be effective, it must be explosive and hard,* almost like a kick. It will be a little difficult to put all the moves together at first, but it will come.

11. The counterattack is with the feet—kick toward the face, groin, or both—whatever is available (Figure 15–46).

12. If you are clear, *take off!* Roll immediately *away* from your opponent until you are on your hands and knees. This maneuver must be done immediately and as fast as possible (Figure 15–47). Then push off like a sprinter coming off the blocks in the 100-yard dash, directly away from your opponent (Figure 15–48). In real life, if you must run *by* your attacker (maybe the only exit is on the other side of him), run by his feet, never his head, where you would be much closer to his reach.

FIGURE 15–43.

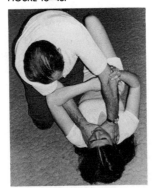

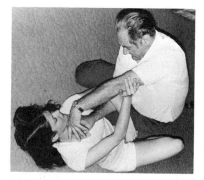

FIGURE 15-44.

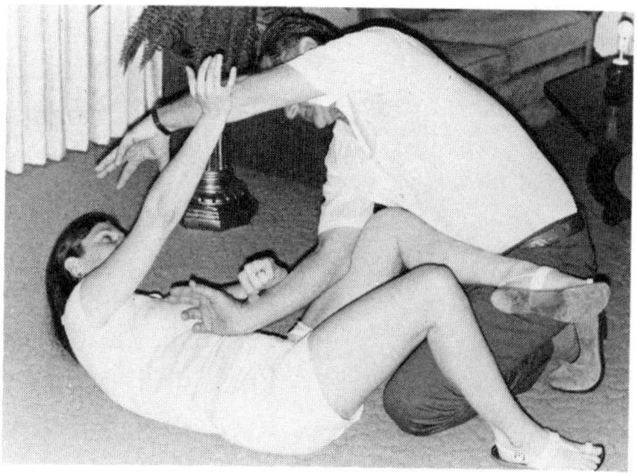

FIGURE 15-45.

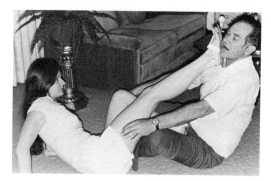

FIGURE 15-46.

FIGURE 15-48.

FIGURE 15-47.

13. In a real-life attack, if you can't get out of the room or to help, run toward a possible weapon and throw something through a window to attract attention. Just for practice, *right now*, look around. If this were for real, what could you use as a weapon and where could you throw something through a window—and what?

(Wherever you are, let your imagination go to work like this occasionally. It's great practice!)

There are a couple of other comments on this technique. If your attacker is too close for you to insert your knee, it may be necessary to distract him by jamming your fingers into his eyes: He will be forced to turn his head and back away slightly, thus giving you a little more room. Be sure to follow up immediately with the knee insert (Surprise *and* Speed, one of your basic principles).

This knee insert is one of the best multi-purpose tricks you can learn and can be used with one or both knees, the second knee giving you much added power. This technique has been used successfully by women while being forced back onto the seat of a car, the leverage of both knees forcing the assailant back and away. This method can be used any time you are on your back or side and the attacker is grabbing you.

Counter to a prone choke

This is when the attacker is not on his knees but is lying full length on top of your body. I'm covering this counter under "strangles," but he may or may not actually be strangling you at this point. He is using his weight to hold you down and is in the position used in an attempted or actual rape. There are two points to remember here. First, he is not overbalanced as he was in the preceding two chokes, and second, your struggles to lift off his dead weight would exhaust you quickly. So, you must keep your cool and think for a second. If he is choking you, you've got to get those hands off of your throat. If he is not choking you, but it is a rape situation, you still have to roll him off you, not only to stop the rape, but also so you can better use

192

your personal weapons and expose more of his vulnerable areas to your attack.

Start the practice by lying on your back. Have your partner lie lengthwise on top of you, *all her weight on you.* She should not be on her knees.

1. Decide which way you are going to roll. The position of the wall or furniture may determine the direction. In setting up the teaching of this counter, I'll have you roll to your left, because that will free your right (strongest) arm for attack. (If you are left-handed, you may prefer to reverse the directions.)

2. With your left hand, reach up around the *outside* of your partner's arm and grab the *outside* of her right shoulder. Jab the heel of your right hand under her left pelvic (hip) bone, grabbing as tightly as you can with your fingers (Figure 15–49).

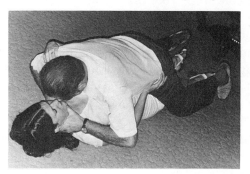

FIGURE 15–49.   FIGURE 15–50.

3. Now you must do *four* things simultaneously: Jam your right leg up to a cocked-leg position as hard and fast as you possibly can, pull straight down with your left hand, thrust up and over with your right hand, and *violently* arch your back and twist over on your left side (Figure 15–50). These moves are designed to upset your attacker's balance and roll him off you. The success of the maneuver is really set up by the kick-like thrust of your cocked leg, using the strongest muscles in your body, the thigh muscles, to lift part of his weight and get him moving so that the other three motions can be effective.

4. At the end of your twist, you will be in about the same position as you were at the end of the counter to the straddle choke, with one possible difference—your opponent may still

FIGURE 15–51.   FIGURE 15–52.

have a choke on you, because nothing you can do is a sure break for a choke in this position. You accomplished all you could, however, which was to bring her into a better position for you to work on the vulnerable areas. *Your first need, however, is to get the hands off your throat.* Because your opponent is not off balance in any direction, and you are not free to maneuver, you will have to finish with the different technique. With your right arm, drive a smashing heel-of-the-hand blow to the outside of her elbow (Figure 15–51). (This is practice, and this blow can injure, so you'll have to simulate it to some extent. Otherwise, your crippled partner's interest in working with you may be a mite diminished.) This blow should drive the hands off your throat. If the first blow doesn't do it, hit again, possibly first driving for the eyes to distract her.

5. As your follow through, drive your fingers to the eyes (Figure 15–52); then use a grasp to the groin. Here is another situation in which where you must hurt him badly in order to get away, because he still has a hold on you. Grab, squeeze, and twist. When he is hurt, release, get up, and run.

COUNTERS TO BODY-LOCKS ("BEAR HUGS")

"Body-lock" is a fancy name for a "bear hug," in which someone wraps his arms around you. They come in four types: from the front, from the back, with the arms free, or with the arms pinned. There are numerous judo- and wrestling-type throws and maneuvers used to counter body-locks, but we will ignore them here, because their use requires extensive training in judo-type throws and falls, which are beyond the province of this book. The majority of them are not practical for the average untrained person, man or woman, so we will concentrate on your personal weapons and his vulnerable areas. This approach does not require the many hours of instruction and degree of skill the other approaches do and if worked properly will give better results.

This approach is usually successful because of the physical position of the attacker. By grabbing you with his two arms, he has removed those same arms from protecting himself from an attack to his vulnerable areas. Even more important, he is unaware of just how vulnerable his vulnerable areas are to the trained woman—you!—so much so that this attack puts you in a better counter-attack position than most other things he could do.

Front body-lock (arms free)

Figure 15–53 shows the obvious weaknesses of the attacker's position. In this particular attack, his arms are usually high and he will squeeze you tightly to his chest to immobilize you. (Is *he* going to be surprised!)

Hand tailor your defenses to the seriousness of the situation. Is it an unwelcome hug at a family party? A hug aimed at

FIGURE 15–53.

immobilizing you so he can give you an unwanted kiss at the end of a date? Or is it the first contact in an attempted rape? I'll merely list the counters you can use. You determine which ones to choose from your arsenal and how hard you want to apply them. Let your conscience, and his aggressiveness, be your guide.

The practicing of these counters gives you an excellent review of vulnerable areas and personal weapons, as well as a fine chance to become proficient in their uses. Go through them all numerous times. You will be setting up those habit-patterns I refer to so often, and the skills will jump to your use in an emergency without any conscious thought on your part at all. (Remember the example I used previously about driving a car?)

Instead of repeating a series of photographs, I want you to refer to Chapters 12 and 13, in which they have already been set out. It will help to go back and reread the directions now.

1. A heel-of-the-hand blow or push under his nose, forcing his head back.

2. Press your thumb under his nose, pushing his head back.

3. Your thumbs dug into his mastoid area.

4. The middle finger dug into the hollow of his throat.

5. A pinch or bite on his trapezius muscle.

6. Your thumb into his eyes. This doesn't have to put his eye out; steady pressure on his eyeball with the *ball* of your thumb will make him back away to relieve the pressure. (Try it on yourself.)

7. Bite whatever is handy—his cheek, ear, trapezius, or chest, depending on your relative heights.

8. If he is holding you low, you can insert your two forearms between your chest and his and push them up under his throat.

9. If he makes the mistake of holding his head back, hitting the top of your forehead to the point or bridge of his nose is very effective.

10. Also, if his head is up, jab your thumbs under his jawbone, pushing upwards.

11. Reach around behind him and grab the back of his hair. Pull *straight down*, not out. This sets up his face and throat for other attacks, such as a heel of the hand under the nose, jab to the eyes, etc.

12. Pull and twist his ears.

13. Scrape the side of your shoes down his shins.

14. Stomp on his toes at the termination of the shin-scrape, two for the price of one. (This is used more for nonlethal social situations.)

15. Knee to the groin.

16. The best and most effective: The grasp to the groin. If your arms are being held high by his arms under your armpits, bending and jerking from side to side will bring one of your hands close enough to the target.

17. Any other attacks you can think of and he makes available.

Front body-lock (arms pinned)

Figure 15–54 shows the relative positions of your bodies with the arms pinned. Note that he has to have his arms much lower in order to successfully pin your arms. With your arms pinned, many of the attacks you could use with the arms free are no longer available, but *he is!*

1. If he is merely an obnoxious masher trying to plant a big kiss on your undesiring lips, a sharp tap of the top of your forehead to his nose or face will end *that* romantic interlude. However, if it is more serious, increase the force of the blow. It will hurt him.

2. Bite! His ear, neck, chest, trapezius muscle—anything within reach.

3. Scrape his shins and stomp his toes.

FIGURE 15–54.

4. Knee to the groin.

5. Look at Figure 15–54. Note the position of the woman's hands! The assailant has set himself up again. Note also that the grasp to the groin should now be used with *both* your hands. (Why be half safe?)

Rear body-lock (arms free)

Figure 15–55 shows the relative positions in this hold. Note that he must hold high in order to immobilize your hands. However, you are absolutely *loaded* with counters!

1. Back of head to nose. Learn to do this automatically whenever you are grabbed from the rear. As soon as the arms come around you, jerk that head back. Most of the time you will feel the arms disappear. His hands will be busy holding his agonized nose! Do this as soon as he makes contact, before he thinks of, or gets around to, burying his head on your shoulder, which any trained man does immediately and the others do a little later. By hitting immediately, you'll catch most of them.

2. Go for the groin grasp. Your hands may be too high because of his high hold under your arms, but if you swing violently from side to side and possibly bend your knees, one hand or the other will come within range of the target. One is all that is necessary.

3. Kick your heel back into his shins.

4. Stomp.

5. Reach over your shoulders with both thumbs, one on each side, and go for his eyes. He may whip his head back and forth

FIGURE 15–55.

to avoid you, or bury it on your shoulder, but keep trying. *You will get it.* Otherwise he'll have to let you go in order to protect his eyes.

6. Reach the ball of your thumb back and get it under his nose and force his head upward.

7. Get the tips of your fingers under his jawbone and push up.

8. Twist his ears.

9. Bang your extended knuckle into the back of his hand. Using the extended knuckles of *both* of your hands to beat a rapid tattoo—sort of like a drumroll—as hard as you can on the back of his hand is extremely effective. The cumulative effect is devastating.

10. Use the finger or thumb peelback (see Figures 15–18 through 15–21, on page 177). If you have practiced these, they will come easy now. Let's set it up for you for practice, however. Let's say your partner's left hand is the one on top of her right arm, as in Figure 15-55. With both hands, work on her forefinger. When it starts to loosen, get the double grip with both hands (use all your muscles), and peel it off.

Rear body-lock (arms pinned)

Figure 15–56 shows this one. Notice that the attacker's arms must be held low in order to hold your arms. Again, your freedom of movement is curtailed more than it was in the preceding body-lock.

FIGURE 15–56.

1. As usual, swing that head back immediately.

2. As minor annoyances, kick back into his shins and stomp his toes.

3. Again, note the photograph (Figure 15–56). Your hands are in position for the usual *piece de resistance*—the grasp to the groin—with *two* hands this time. Squeeze hard! His arms should open. Hang on with one hand, turn *in* to him, and deliver any of your personal weapons, such as the heel of the hand under his nose.

COUNTERS TO A REAR ARM-STRANGLE

For our purposes, consider the rear arm-strangle as a body-lock from the rear with the arms free (Figure 15–57). This is also known as the mugging hold and is very common in purse snatchings and other robbery attempts. Unlike the body-lock defenses, there is that three-second deadline we use on any strangle situation, so you must move fast.

One thing you can do as a preliminary technique if his forearm is crushing your windpipe is to grab the strangling arm with both your hands and pull down while you turn your head toward the crook of the arm (Figure 15–58). This will ease the pressure by putting your windpipe in the open space inside his bent elbow.

FIGURE 15–57.

FIGURE 15–58.

FIGURE 15–59.

FIGURE 15–60.   FIGURE 15–61.

From here, we go into the various counter-attacks. An upward-sweeping thumb to his eyes (Figure 15–59) or a two-handed groin grasp (Figure 15–60) would be about the most effective weapon here. If your assailant is too well trained for you to get to, suddenly go *completely limp* as if you had passed out. Try to drop to the ground (Figure 15–61). It is your only chance. The chances are he'll let go or maybe even lose his hold on you, as a suddenly limp body is almost impossible to hold unless one is braced for it. Then, when you are free of the strangle, await your opportunity to flee or counter attack.

COUNTERS TO A HEADLOCK

The headlock is a convenient wrestling technique that can be used to hold you helpless, inflict punishment, or drag you off to some spot that your attacker likes better. Depending on the seriousness of the situation (it is often used by a boyfriend in a friendly tussle), you can use one of several counters.

1. If the situation is not lethal: Have your partner get you into a headlock with her right arm. With your inside hand (the left in this case), reach between her legs and administer a firm

FIGURE 15–62.

pinch on the tender flesh on the inside of her right thigh, about two-thirds of the way up from her knee (Figure 15–62). (Do this gently, or you will have a very irate partner.) The secret here is that the inside of the thigh is *very* tender, and most people will jump a foot and let go. Your boyfriend will not be very happy with this one either, but it works. In the case of a vicious attack, use it, but your victim might not let go. The pinch here is not a crippler, but it might distract him and make your next move easier.

2. Another less-than-lethal counter, but one that can be used in either a playful romp with your boyfriend or an actual attack, is

FIGURE 15–63.   FIGURE 15–64.

FIGURE 15–65.

FIGURE 15–66.

the hair pull. Have your partner put you into a headlock. Slide your *inside* hand up the middle of her back (Figure 15–63), get a good grip on her hair (use the correct technique as explained previously), and pull the hair straight down her back. This will cause her to arch her back and either let go of your head or fall down. In a real attack, the arching of the back should expose the groin to a blow or grasp. (Figure 15–64).

3. This one is more complicated, but it is actually easy once you understand it. Have your partner get you into a headlock with her right arm. Swing your inside arm (in this case your left) backward and up over the top of her near shoulder, your palm toward her face and your thumb on the bottom (Figure 15–65). Put the inside bone of your thumb under the base of her nose and roll her head back over her spine (Figure 15–66). If this does not work, have your partner help you get the proper pressure on that bone under her nose (if necessary, refer to page 147 and Figure 12–1). This one takes a little practice, but once you get it, it will be very effective. If this were a real attack, the assailant will be arched over backward, exposing the groin area as described in step 2.

4. In a lethal attack, go for the groin, either between your opponent's legs with your inside hand or around the front with your outside hand, or both.

COUNTERS TO A
HAMMER-LOCK

I'm including counters to this hold because it is often used to immobilize a woman. A man finds this very easy to apply to a weaker woman. You've seen the hold many times on TV and in professional wrestling. It merely means that your arm is twisted up behind your back (Figure 15–67). It is very painful and could be crippling if your assailant wanted it to be, but it does not make the situation hopeless by any means. The main thing you have going for you here is that he doesn't expect you to be able to do anything about it. Actually, not too many men know the counters to the hammerlock. Let's have your long-suffering partner put you in a hammerlock.

The first counter is used if you are being held close to his body. Think! What does this remind you of? You're right! It is about the same as a body-lock from the rear. He has set himself up again! Reach back with your free hand and get a tight grasp on the groin (Figure 15–68). He'll let go! Maintaining that grasp if you can, turn in to your opponent and strike a heel-of-the-hand blow to the base of the nose, and, if you care to, follow up with a knee to the groin (Figure 15–69) or a top-of-the-head smash to the nose and/or a knee to the groin (Figure 15–70).

If your wrist isn't locked (you'll know if it is), you must do several things simultaneously in the second counter:

1. Jam your captured right wrist toward the floor as you execute a downward-spiralling turn toward your bent elbow, bending

FIGURE 15–67.

FIGURE 15–68.

FIGURE 15–69.

FIGURE 15–70.

your knees as you go. With your left foot, step slightly forward and across your body (Figure 15–71).

2. As you continue your turn, straighten your elbow as much as you can to relieve the pressure on it (Figure 15–72). This will also bring you in closer to your opponent for your counterattack.

3. Complete the turn as far as possible, trying to come face to face with your opponent. Counterattack with a groin grasp or blow; from this position he can't see it coming (Figure 15–73).

It is particularly important to take your opponent by surprise in this counter, as the key to its success is your ability to partially straighten your arm in step 1. It will probably be necessary to set up your surprise by aiming a blow or grasp at

FIGURE 15–71.

FIGURE 15–72.

FIGURE 15–73.

the groin. Even if you don't succeed, it will distract him long enough for you to get in that first move.

COUNTERS TO HAIR PULLING

If we can believe the caveman cartoons, it has been traditional from time immemorial for women to be hauled around by the hair. But traditional or not, a grip on your hair can be not only painful but also controlling, as there are few better handles with which to drag you around. There are several effective counters for this, however, depending upon how you are being gripped.

1. If the assailant is facing you and grabs the top of your hair with his right hand (Figure 15–74), immediately lock first your left hand and then your right hand on top of his and press them down as tightly as possible to the top of your head (Figure 15–75). His attempts to pull your hair will fail, because the pull has been transferred to your hands. He can still pull you around, but without pain to you, and therefore without as much control. (*Try it!*)

By releasing your top hand, you still maintain your protective grip on his hand with your lower hand but have the top hand free to attack whatever vulnerable areas you deem it practical and advisable to attack under the circumstances (Figure 15–76). Try it with your partner. Now you see why we placed the right hand on top: When it's released for attack, his vulnerable areas become wide open. If you had used the other hand on top, you would have few targets.

FIGURE 15–74.

FIGURE 15-75.

FIGURE 15-76.

2. If he grabs the top of your hair *from behind* (Figure 15–77), again lock your two hands over his (Figure 15–78) and whirl into him (Figure 15–79), releasing your top hand for active duty against whatever targets you choose (Figure 15–80). In combat

FIGURE 15-77.

FIGURE 15-78.

FIGURE 15-79.

FIGURE 15-80.

FIGURE 15–81.

FIGURE 15–82.

FIGURE 15–83.

FIGURE 15–84.

FIGURE 15–85.

the suddenness and speed of your whirl should really surprise the devil out of him, making him an easy target for your first attack.

3. If he grabs the ends of your hair from behind (Figure 15–81), simply whirl into him (Figure 15–82) as above and counterattack (Figure 15–83).

4. If he pulls your hair correctly, i.e., pulls it straight down your back, snapping your head back (Figure 15–84), drop down suddenly to relieve the pressure and whirl toward him in a down spiral (Figure 15–85) counterattacking as indicated.

COUNTER TO BLOWS
AND KICKS

I'm going to disappoint some of you on this one because I'm not going to include the usual self-defense methods of blocking kicks with the side of your foot, crossed arms, parry and lift, and so on, nor against blows by the numerous boxing parries, slapoffs, and wrap-arounds. If you want those, go to the library or book store and pull out some of the other books on self-defense. Or better yet, take one off the body of a woman who tried to use one of those techniques on a competent man. She won't be using it again. I'm not being facetious. Even a trained boxer can't ward off all blows, nor can a really trained and fast man avoid all kicks. Trying to teach these very specialized and difficult techniques from a book is ridiculous. A long course in judo, karate, kung fu, or some of the other martial arts might help, but you will need much training and practice. So I'm not going to waste our time and give you a false feeling of security in something that I know from experience won't work. I can only give you a couple of common-sense rules that might put you in a position in which you *can* do something about it.

To start with, the average woman—or man, for that matter—when under attack by an adversary who is swinging his fists or feet, always tries to back away, while fending off the attack with her arms (Figure 15–86). Wrong! This merely allows the attacker to continue until one of his blows lands. You are doing nothing to either stop the attacker or escape. Let an attacker deliver enough unopposed swings and kicks without

FIGURE 15–86.

209

retaliation and he could cripple King Kong. Also, he can move faster going forward than you can moving backward. Even if you turn and run, the chances are that he can outrun you and will continue his attack, so there is no future in retreat in most cases. The common-sense rule is that if you can't escape, don't back away, but instead *move in* close to your opponent. I know this one will be hard for you to accept at first, as it goes completely against your normal instinct, which is to run from danger. Trust me! To protect yourself as much as possible from his blows as you move in, you must cover your vulnerable areas and make yourself as small a target as possible. Close both fists, jam your knuckles into your forehead at about the hairline, put your chin on your chest, keep your elbows together (grab your hair to lock your hands in place if you want), and bend forward slightly at the waist (Figure 15–87). *Rush* into your opponent. *Keep your eyes open* and peek through your covering arms as you go in; otherwise he will simply sidestep, let you rush blindly by, and clobber you. As you move in, his blows will be on the top of your head and forearms; this is not exactly fun, but far superior to being hit in the face, breasts, or stomach. Wrap your arms around his torso and bury your head on his shoulder (Figure 15–88). *Plaster* yourself against him, hugging him tightly. This leaves him very few vulnerable areas to work on and forces him to use short, relatively ineffective blows on your back. He can't get a good swing (and he can't kick you at all!). This approximates what a professional boxer does—going into a "clinch"—when he can't cope with his opponent's attack. If it's good enough for the professional, it's good enough for you.

FIGURE 15–87.

FIGURE 15–88.

FIGURE 15–89.

Now for the good news: Look at your position. You are in the same situation as in a body-lock from the front and are now in close enough to use your personal weapons against his vulnerable areas. With surprise, you have a good chance of turning the tables, which is a lot better chance than you had before. If you don't know what vulnerable areas to go for and what personal weapons to use by this time, you just haven't been paying attention. Go back to square one (in this case, page one). Do not collect $200.

This protective stance is effective when standing, and a variation will help if you are down and someone is hitting or kicking you. Use the same hand and arm positions and draw your legs up tight against your chest, like in the fetal position (Figure 15–89). You are less vulnerable in this position than in any other if you are helpless. It is also a good position if someone is trying to rape you or tear your clothes off. It is extremely difficult for anyone to get at you. Of course, you are always looking for a chance to get away or to surprise your attacker with a counter-attack.

COUNTER TO BITES

This counter applies to any bite, whether it be by a human, dog, or wild animal. (By the way, if you are bitten by a human and the skin is broken, go to a doctor and get a tetanus shot.

The bite from a human is far more likely to become infected than any other kind.) But back to counters. The usual reaction to a bite is to pull away, but if the biter is sincere about it, you won't be able to pull loose. You are playing into his strength. Instead, whether it be a hand, arm, wrist, or leg, jam the part being bitten as hard as you can directly back into the hinge of his jaws. If anything will open the jaws, this will, and in any case it will prevent him from biting any harder. *Try it!* Have a partner bite you lightly on your forearm or hand. Now, *gently* push that forearm or hand straight back to the hinge of the jaw. Your partner will back off quickly enough. Then reverse the procedure so that you can feel how effective it is.

You will note that the pressure was against the very muscles that are used to furnish power to the jaws, which prevents further closing; that it causes pain, which will force him to relinquish his grip; and that, as he is forced backward to relieve the pressure, he is set up for one of your clever and deadly counter-attacks. If you try to jerk away, particularly from an animal, the chances are that his canine teeth will slash your flesh. The forward pressure blocks this unpleasant happening.

You can add to the biter's discomfort by the use of any personal weapons that come to mind. Digging your fingers under his jawbone may be helpful, but his eyes are the closest vulnerable areas, so put pressure on his eyeball with your thumb. He'll have to let go. Depending upon where you are being bitten, use the appropriate weapon.

CHAPTER SIXTEEN
CONCLUSION

Although this is the conclusion of the book, it should be just the beginning for you. If you now put it down, merely regarding it as interesting reading, it has not accomplished its purpose, and one of the bad guys may conclude you! There must be a follow-through that will continue the rest of your life (which then has a far better chance of being long). The foregoing chapters are a compendium of the dos and don'ts of self-protection and self-defense, but only a compendium. There are many thousands of other ideas, techniques, and procedures limited only by the situation and your imagination. The value of this book depends entirely upon how seriously you take the instruction. If you *do* follow the procedures set forth in its first half, which details the preventive side of the problem, the possibility of your becoming an unpleasant police statistic is remote. The methods set forth to accomplish this happy state of affairs are based on common-sense precautions that must be applied realistically, but must be applied all the time.

So you now possess the means of preventing most of the terrifying happenings that could wreck or even end your life and of preventing the loss of valuable and irreplaceable property. *But*—you have to use those means. The case of seat belts presents a good analogy. We know they save the lives of a great percentage of those who use them, but we also know that simply installing them in your car will not protect you. You must buckle them on (a terrible nuisance that takes all of five seconds!). Many drivers, because they are impatient or have listened to some big-mouth claiming that seat belts kill more people than they save (a bunch of unmitigated garbage, by the way) deliberately do not use them, and several thousand die horribly or suffer agonizing and crippling injuries each year as a result. Police records are full of reports about people who died unnecessarily when they were pitched out of their cars in minor

fender-bender accidents because they thought seat belts were a nuisance or because they were "only going to the store." They *died* to save five seconds!

So it is with the safety precautions set forth herein. Unless you use them every time—*every time*—you may become a victim. They must become part of your everyday living pattern. Discuss them with other people; it will help to set them in your mind. Role play the various situations that might occur so that you get the practice of deciding your probable actions. You will become remarkably adept and far more likely to react effectively in an emergency. Make up your mind—*right now*—to start following the rules. Remember that if you fail to follow the rules some of the time because "it's just for a minute," it's exactly the same as not putting on the seat belt because you are "just going to the store." You can *die* because of it.

The second half of the book sets out practical physical methods to escape the eager clutches of your attacker. These methods make interesting reading and are great for fantasizing about all the terrible and painful things you're going to do to him if you are attacked. Forget it! Unless you have painstakingly worked on the methods step by step, they are not likely to do you much good in a panic-prone emergency situation. Are you really serious about your safety? Learn the methods over a period of time, in slow motion at first, and exactly as I set them out. If they are not working properly, have someone help you, because you are doing something wrong. They *do* work! After you have mastered them, have your partner be more aggressive and catch you by surprise more often. When you think you are pretty good, practice on a male partner, but pick one who is mature enough to help and not try to demonstrate what a weak and helpless species the female is and how strong he is. It is a good idea to explain to him what you are trying to accomplish and what is expected of him. Especially point out that surprise is lacking. This stress/combat training will really sharpen your skills. Here you will learn the advantage of hesitating a moment to collect your thoughts instead of exploding immediately in a panic reaction.

If you have followed the preventive steps, however, you will probably never need the physical techniques. And if you have learned the physical techniques and *do* need to use them, is *he* going to be surprised!!

INDEX